GOOD ADVICE

ABCs for People
Who Don't Have All the Answers

Jim Hancock and Todd Temple
Illustrated by C. McNair Wilson

Grow For It Books

Published by Youth Specialties, Inc.
El Cajon, California

GOOD ADVICE: ABC'S FOR PEOPLE WHO DON'T HAVE ALL THE ANSWERS

Grow For It Books are published by Youth Specialties, Inc. 1224 Greenfield Drive, El Cajon, CA 92021.

© 1987 by Youth Specialties, Inc.

Library of Congress Cataloging-in-Publication Data

Hancock, Jim, 1952-
  Good advice.

  (Grow for it books)
  Summary: Information and guidance on a variety of topics (abortion, accountability, addiction, adolescence, adoption, AIDS, alcohol, anger, arguing, etc.), from a Christian perspective, listed alphabetically.
  1. Youth—Religious life. 2. Youth—Conduct of life. [1. Conduct of life. 2. Christian life] I. Temple, Todd, 1958- . II Wilson, C. McNair, ill. III. Title. IV. Series.
BV4531.2.H3 1987   248.8'3   87-29551
ISBN 0-910125-09-0

Edited by Wayne Rice and Tim McLaughlin
Illustrations by C. McNair Wilson

Printed in the United States of America

First printing 1987

INTRODUCTION

Good Advice isn't the last word on anything—just our best thoughts on some things that matter (and, perhaps, a few that don't). We hope you'll read with your eyes wide open—ask questions, doubt our word, think new thoughts.

Let's start with true confessions. If you knew us, you might take this good advice with a grain of salt. We're a couple of youth workers with word processors and courage (or gall) enough to hope we can add some perspective to your changing world.

Just like you, we've needed and gotten some good

advice through the years. Some we took, some we didn't. We survived our worst mistakes, learned from them, and in some ways this little book is our way of saying, "If I knew then what I know now, this is probably what I'd have done."

We're sorry this couldn't be *Great Advice*. We just didn't have it in us. And, of course, it couldn't be *Best Advice*. That book has already been written, and our acknowledgement to its Author is on every page of this work.

Have fun!

Jim Hancock
Todd Temple

ACKNOWLEDGEMENTS

In a way, *Good Advice* is a tribute to the wonderful folks who've given themselves, along with their advice, to us through the years: Katie Temple, for believing in the unbelievable; Susan and Kate Hancock, for the great hug-a-war; our parents, for not drowning us when they had the chance—teaching us, instead, to swim; Tom Julian and Jim Burns, for advice lived before spoken; the Camp Fox team; the folks at Youth Specialties, for helping us dream; John Emmans, for "The Knowledge of the Holy"; the Dawn Patrol (and friends); and The Lion.

We also acknowledge our debt to the dozens of writers, teachers, pastors, speakers, and friends from whom we've learned our best material. We tried to give credit where credit was due and have not intentionally omitted anyone. If you feel slighted, we're sorry. Call us—we'll do lunch.

I need good advice—a word to the wise,
Illumination to my eyes.
I need good friends, not prone to pretend—
Lord, they give me that good advice.

Well, it's common sense, shared without pretense,
Honest opinions, in love without offense.
Sometimes it can be an angle you don't see,
And if you're asking me, I'll try to make it be

A little bit of good advice—a word to the wise,
Illumination to my eyes.
I need good friends, not prone to pretend—
Lord, you give me that good advice.

—James Ward

ABBA

You can spell *Abba* in either direction and end up with the same word.

But *Abba* is no ordinary reversible word; it's very special to us.

We don't use *Abba* very often—that's because we're not Jewish. *Abba* is a Hebrew word that means *daddy*. It's one of the first words a Jewish baby speaks, like "Da-da!"

When Jesus taught his disciples to pray, he said, "Start your prayers like this: Our Father (Abba) who lives in heaven . . . " People thought he was kidding around. They usually called God something like, "O Great King, Master of the Universe, Thou Exalted One Who created the Heavens and the Earth . . . " And they wore suits and ties when they said it.

But Jesus said to call God your daddy because that's what he is. If he had a baseball glove, he'd want to play catch with you. If he had a wallet, your picture would be in it. He loves you and he loves the sound of your voice when you see him coming: "Daddy!"

If you're looking for a good religion, God can't help you much because he's not after *followers*. He's after sons and daughters, and he aims to make one out of any creature who dares to believe that this good news is as good as it sounds.

And from here in, anybody who is a son or daughter of God is authorized and encouraged to call him *dad*. It's the freshest, most intimate family reference there is: Abba. Daddy.

It's *too* intimate for some—they think God ought to keep his distance, maintain his dignity as befits the head of a religion.

Thankfully, our Abba does what *he* wants to do!

Whenever you feel alone, afraid, or messed up, remember that God is your daddy. You can crawl up on his lap and tell him about it. He'll listen and understand and comfort and help.

That's the best advice we can give to begin *Good Advice*.

See: God, Jesus.

ABORTION

Abortion is a fighting word for a lot of people. So let's set aside the subject for a minute and talk about the cause of teenage abortions: sex. Will you have sexual intercourse before you're married? Yes or no? You pick.

YES

"Yes" means a world of maybe's, some likely, some extremely remote. Maybe venereal disease. Maybe AIDS. (Maybe you'll just *worry* about contracting a disease.)

Maybe you'll get the feeling that you've experienced something intensely beautiful, yet curiously lacking in one feature. At first glance you don't know what's wrong, but when you discover the missing piece, just the knowledge of its absence seems to turn the whole image into something grotesque. Like looking at a beautiful body with no head or a stillborn kitten. Or maybe you'll never even notice that something is missing, thinking that life is as good as it gets when it's mediocre.

Maybe you'll get pregnant (or maybe you'll get her

pregnant). And maybe you'll get an abortion. Maybe you'll damage your uterus and cash in your chances for a child with your husband. Maybe you'll get that sick feeling that somehow the "tissue" inside you (or her) was human, and you put an end to someone's life. Maybe you'll spend years (or your life) sorting out the reason why half the population says it's wrong and the other half says it isn't, and not knowing which half to believe. Maybe you'll wonder how cheap and easy it was to initiate the one process that makes you most like God (the ability to create life), and then stop it mid-course with a vacuum. Or maybe none of these thoughts will ever cross your mind. Maybe that's better. Maybe that's worse.

NO

"No" means that you make an unpopular choice, a lonely stand, a frustrating wait, a wild risk that somehow all the maybe's aren't worth it and that God and his ways *are*. Your not-before-marriage says no to a process that *starts out* wrong. And for nearly half a million teenage girls each year (and, of course, for that many guys), the process ends in an abortion. At best, abortion is a gross abuse of God's gift of reproduction; at worst, it's *far* worse.

If you're a partner to a pregnancy, you have some extremely tough choices to make. Talk over your dilemma and your options with a parent, church worker, or other trusted adult. One organization that can help you is called Birthright. They have centers all over the world, and you can find one near you by looking their name up in your phone book. (If you can't find it, call their main office in Toronto at 416/469-1111.) Another group of people who are committed to helping you with abortion alternatives is

Bethany Christian Services—their national hotline is 1-800-BETHANY.

See: Pregnancy, Safe Sex, Technical Virginity.

ACCOUNTABILITY

When you give someone the right to demand something from you, you're *accountable* to them. You're accountable to your teachers if they can demand work from you and expect you to deliver. You're accountable to your parents if they expect you to perform certain responsibilities and behave in a

particular way. Accountability is a good thing because it gives others a say in how you live your life—left on your own you're likely to make lots of bad choices. And when you know that someone else is expecting something of you and that he will be disappointed if you fail to deliver, you're motivated to do better.

Two important facts about accountability:

You give someone the right to hold you accountable. If you live at home, you give your parents the right to expect you in by a certain hour. And if you don't come home in time, your folks are authorized to punish you. You never signed a permission form, but it's part of the package deal you agree to by choosing to live at home.

By choosing to be a part of a church, you give the other members of the church permission to expect certain things from you. That doesn't mean they have the right to run your life, but it does mean that other believers can encourage you, point out danger zones, and—if they need to—tell you that you're not living right.

When you call someone a friend (and if he really is one), you give him the right to tell you when you're messing up. But it also means that you agree to listen to what he has to say, even if it hurts. "Wounds from a friend can be trusted, but an enemy multiplies kisses."[1]

Accountability is mutual. There's a great sense of security when you know that someone out there cares if you make it home tonight. It's nice to know that you have friends who will whack you on the side of the head with the truth should you start to drift off to la-la land. Our hope is that you have friends and family members who give you that sense of security by holding you accountable. If you do, be sure to give them the same feeling by holding *them* accountable. First, encourage them often. Second, pray for them.

Third, be honest with them in the most loving way you can. (See Friendship for more ideas on how to do this.) Although a person's actions are ultimately her own responsibility, you share in the responsibility of keeping her safe, loved, and on the right track if she is a part of your family, church, or friendship group.

If you feel like you're living without the safety net of accountability, tell someone. Find someone you can trust, and give them permission to expect the right kind of behavior and attitude from you. But prepare yourself for some friendly wounds.

More: Proverbs 11:14; 27:17; Galatians 6:2.

[1]Proverbs 27:6.

ADOLESCENCE

Never be ashamed of what you are. By the way, what *are* you? A kid, a teen, a young person, a youth, an adolescent, a young adult? In its turn, each identity is annoying because it fails to capture the fact that you're a person—changing, growing, already complete in the way a rosebud is complete, which yet opens up to reveal hidden and developing petals.

Our culture has both good news and bad news for people hung out there between childhood and . . . what? The good news is that we generally acknowledge the changing nature of life in these years and try to buffer kids from the responsibilities of marriage, making a living, fighting wars, and so on. The bad news is that people are segregated by age to the extent that we seldom spend much time in *real* relationships with anybody who's not pretty close to our own age. Adults apparently expect that a fourteen-year-old will learn maturity from television, movies, and other fourteen-year-olds. Not realistic. Not fair.

Some more not-so-good news (sorry): nobody is likely to do a lot to change this while you're still an adolescent. So if anything is to be done, you'll have to

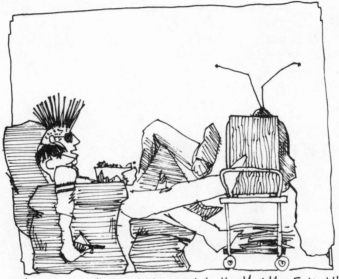

"I'm sure glad your folks went to the Mad Max Festival!"
"Yah! They never let me watch the Mickey Mouse Club."

do it. But that's good news! Adolescence is a phase of becoming—becoming a man or woman in mind, body, emotion, spirit, and relationship with your world. The process looks a little different on each person, so if you take the initiative to guide your own adolescence, to find the relational resources you need to get to maturity ASAP, who is going to say that's not terrific?

Why not build relationships with mature people around you—not just two years or five years, but ten, twenty, fifty years older. There are teachers, youth workers, retired people from whom you can learn. They can learn from you, too. (In fact, you know you've got a match if you can listen to each other for more than a few minutes.) Find one or two people who fit the bill, and make a way to spend a few hours together every month. You probably already know him/her but just need to find the right activity to make your relationship grow.

More: Luke 2:52.

See: Private Parts.

ADOPTION

When you're adopted, there's bad news and there's good news. The bad news is that, for some reason you'll never really know, your biological parents allowed you to be raised by someone else. For most people that's a hard pill to swallow. "Why would they do that?" you wonder. "My mother carried me for nine months, for crying out loud! Why would they bail out on me? What was wrong with them? What was wrong with me?"

Those are tough questions made tougher by the fact that there are no answers for most of them.

But there is an answer to the last question. *Nothing!* There was nothing wrong with you. Whatever the reason, it had nothing to do with you. In fact, they didn't even know you.

Which leads us to the good news. Someone—your parents—adopted you. *You.* They took the calculated risk of bringing you into their family. It was no accident. They meant to do it. That's exciting!

God uses the imagery of adoption to describe his free choice of you and me as children for his heavenly family. Nobody forces God to adopt you. He does it because he wants to. In some ways, it may be easier for an adopted child to grasp that. In other ways, it's as difficult for adopted people to accept as it is for anyone else.

If you find yourself asking uncomfortable questions, don't stop—keep asking them. Even if there are no answers, it's good to voice the questions.

More: Ephesians 1:3-5.

AIDS

Let's not talk about it.

AIDS

It's not a very nice subject.

AIDS

Okay. We'll talk about it.

AIDS isn't a homosexual disease. The sexual habits of homosexual men make them more efficient transmitters of the virus, so about two-thirds of the known cases in the U.S. are homosexual men. But about twenty-five percent of the cases are drug addicts who share needles, and one out of every ten victims got the virus through heterosexual sex, an unsafe blood transfusion, an infected mother, or some undetermined method.

Acquired Immune Deficiency Syndrome is a nasty disease because it attacks the very protection system that's in your body to fight off disease. So when another virus comes along (pneumonia, for example, or meningitis), your antibodies are nowhere to be found. Your body is defenseless — a country without an army. As of this writing, a cure for the disease has not been found. Those with AIDS have very little chance of survival; many die within months of discovering they have it.

Some people claim that AIDS is God's judgment against sin. They're right. All bad things are a part of God's judgment of a sinful world. Sin entered the world when Adam and Eve rebelled against God — the consequences were banishment from the garden and the reality of pain, disease, and death. Since we have done no better than those two when it comes down to obedience to God, we are partly to blame for the evil around us. But when people claim that AIDS is God's *special* judgment on the sin of homosexuality, we can't agree.

Yes, sin has its consequences, and sexual sin increases your chances for getting a sexually transmitted disease. But if AIDS is the punishment for homosexuality, then it would appear that God is practicing sex discrimination, since very few lesbian women have AIDS. He must also be getting the names mixed up, because many gay men don't have AIDS, while children born to mothers with AIDS and blood recipients are being "punished" in their stead.

Christians can use their knowledge of Scripture to show people that Christ's love is greater than sin and disease. The Bible says that every one of us is a sinner. Some of us commit sins that make headlines; others rebel against God in more socially acceptable ways. "We all, like sheep, have gone astray, each of us has turned to his own way; [yet] the Lord has laid on [Jesus] the iniquity of us all."[1] The good news for the homosexual and the AIDS victim is the same good news for you: "For the wages of sin is death, but the gift of God is eternal life through Christ Jesus our Lord."[2] Respected pastor and Bible teacher Ray Stedman puts it this way: "The world says to the victim of AIDS, 'You made your bed, now lie in it.' But Jesus' words to him are, 'Rise, take up your bed, and walk.' "

Here are a few commonly asked questions and answers about AIDS:

How do you get AIDS? Mostly by having sex with an infected person or by sharing needles and syringes used to inject drugs. The AIDS virus can exist in the blood, semen, and vaginal secretions of an infected person. It can be transmitted from one homosexual partner to another as well as during sexual intercourse or oral sex between a man and a woman. The virus can enter the body through sores in the mouth and through microscopic tears in the tissue of sex organs.

How else is AIDS transmitted? Some victims were exposed to the AIDS virus through a blood transfusion. Since the start of careful blood screening, this rarely occurs now. About a third of the babies born to mothers with AIDS are infected.

Can you get AIDS from shaking hands, hugging, kissing, French kissing, crying, coughing, sneez-

ing, or eating food prepared by someone with AIDS? Can you get it through masturbation? Can you get it from toilet seats, doorknobs, eating utensils, or insect bites? No known cases have been transmitted in any of these ways. The virus is really fragile outside the body, usually dying within seconds of contact with the outside air.

Can you get AIDS by having your ears pierced? No one is known to have become infected with AIDS in this way as yet, but it's conceivable. If you're having this done, insist on a sterile needle.

Can you get AIDS from someone who doesn't know he or she has it? Yes. This is usually what happens. Because it takes five or more years after exposure for symptoms to appear, most carriers don't discover they have it until they have already passed it on.

Can you be infected with the AIDS virus and never get AIDS? Yes. Although between one-fourth and one-half of those infected with the virus will develop AIDS within four to ten years (some say that the percentage is even higher), not all who are infected will contract the disease.

How can I protect myself from getting AIDS? Wait until marriage before having sex. When you have sexual intercourse or oral sex with someone, you are having sex with everyone your partner has had sex with for the past ten years. Sleeping around is deadly and foolish.

Where can I find out more about AIDS? Your local Red Cross office carries information, as do local and state health departments.

AIDS is such a new crisis, that more is being discovered each week regarding its danger, transmission, and treatment, so this information is likely to be

inadequate soon after it's published. If you are interested in learning more, look for current materials on
the subject.

  [1]Isaiah 53:6.
  [2]Romans 6:23.

ALCOHOL

Deciding if you as teenager should drink is a tough
choice. Here are some questions to ask yourself:

Is your drinking illegal? Drinking ages were
established because people learned the hard way that

alcohol is deadlier for adolescents than for adults. Your body learns habits and addictions quicker, and a smaller body weight means less alcohol is needed to mess up your system.

Does your drinking displease God? While the Bible has some pretty positive things to say about alcohol, it comes down hard on drunkenness. Let's face reality here: for many high schoolers, getting drunk isn't the problem—it's the *goal*. (As one student explained it, "Why *else* would I put something that tastes like that into my mouth?")

Does your drinking put others at risk? Unfortunately, just a little bit of alcohol goes a long way toward messing up your driving. Two beers (or two ounces of hard liquor) and your driving is affected—and that's assuming you're a good driver *without* beer. Three beers (or three mixed drinks) and—depending on your weight, tolerance, and a dozen other factors—you might be either a road hazard or a homicide waiting for a place to happen. (See 502.)

Does your drinking control you in any way? Does it change the kinds of friends you have, how you act, how well you do in school, your relationship with God, how you get along at home, or your health?

If you've just started drinking but want to stop, now is the time. Spend your free time around people who don't drink, and plan fun things to do that don't involve drinking. If drinking has already become a big problem—or you're not sure if it has or not—talk to someone you trust. A pastor, church worker, school counselor, or teacher can either help you or lead you to someone who can.

If someone you care about has a problem with alcohol, call Alcoholics Anonymous in your area and ask them what you can do.

More: Psalm 104:14-15; Proverbs 20:1, 23:20-21, 29-35; John 2:1-10; Ephesians 5:18.

See: Addiction, Materialism, Substance Abuse.

ANGER

Anger is okay. The problem is, most of us get angry about the wrong things. We get angry at unimportant issues and learn to tolerate the things that *should* make us mad. If some people got as angry about world hunger as they did about getting stuck in traffic, there might be a few less hungry people. And

if others showed as much hatred for their own sinfulness as they did for cleaning up their rooms, there would be a lot more godly men and women in high school.

The prophet Amos tells us to "Hate evil, love good."[1] The Apostle Paul explains it this way: "Love must be sincere. Hate what is evil; cling to what is good."[2] Steve Taylor put it in a song: "I just wanna be angry at the evil, I just wanna be hungry for the true."[3] You can see how Steve echoes the Scripture in its pairing of love and hatred: love without hatred is superficial, and hatred without love is bitter. The trick is to remember what to love and what to hate.

If anger is an easy emotion for you, find something evil and hate it—for goodness's sake. If your anger

controls you more than you know it should, find ways to cool off: beat up your pillow, run a mile, read a *Far Side* book, write out your feelings on paper, ask a friend for permission to unload on him, count to ten, take five deep breaths, pray for someone else, go for a walk, or read a travel brochure on Tahiti.

More: Matthew 5:22; Ephesians 4:26.

[1]Amos 5:15.
[2]Romans 12:9.
[3]"I Just Wanna Know," *On the Fritz* (Sparrow).

ANOREXIA

See: Eating Disorders.

ARGUING

If you want to persuade someone to agree with you, arguing is one of the poorest ways to do it. But if you do find yourself in an argument and you haven't so lost your head that you can't think straight, try some of these arguing techniques.

How to argue:
• Don't cut the other speaker off in the middle of a point (unless she has been talking nonstop since yesterday).

• If your partner insists on cutting you off, tell him that you allowed him to finish his point and you expect the same courtesy. If he continues to cut you off, stick a sock in his mouth.

• Speak in a normal voice. A calm, steady voice suggests clear thinking.

• Argue one point at a time. If your partner skirts a point, come back to it.

• Don't make ad hominem (Latin for *to the man*) statements, which are those that attack your partner instead of the issue (e.g., "How would you know, zipper head?"). Ignore ad hominems made against you. (But if he starts saying things about your mother, go for blood.)

• Try listening to what the other person says. If she senses that you're really considering her words, she'll think more carefully before saying something.

• If you lose, surrender! The issue isn't *who* is right, but *what* is right.

• Remember, the best argument for your view is that you obviously care more for your adversary—for whom Christ died—than you do for winning the argument.

How to stop an argument:
• Walk away.
• Imagine, in relation to the universe, how absolutely ridiculous the disagreement is.
• Agree with her.
• Pay her to agree with you.
• If the argument is serious and requires resolution, invite a third party to judge between you.

More: James 1:19.

See: Anger.

BORING

Four guys sat on the front step at Mike's house for three and a half hours one July night repeating the litany of summer: "What do you want to do?"

"I don't know—what do *you* want to do?"

"I don't know . . . "

Quick now—were they bored?

No! In fact, they had a great time fooling around, telling stories, and remembering other good times.

After a while, the way to get a laugh and start the next round of stories was to ask, "So, what do you want to do?"

Boredom is the weariness and discontent that results from having too much of something (Health ed., Sunday school, time on your hands) or from plain disinterest. There's an SAT word you can look up to help you understand boredom—it's *ennui* (pronounced ON-wee.) The solution to boredom is to stay on your toes so you never get a bellyful of ennui. (Now you *have* to look it up!) If that sounds impossible, perhaps you underestimate your potential for creating your own fun.

Only You Can Prevent Boredom. Here are some ideas:

• Keep something good to read close at hand.
• Ask a stranger what people in these parts do for fun.
• Rub your eyes and say out loud, "Did you see that?"
• Write a stupid poem about what you're doing. ("I think that I could never pass/A subject taught within this class.")
• Write an anonymous note and hide it where no one will ever find it—but if someone does, it will make her laugh hysterically and wonder for the rest of her life.
• Make lists of things to do, places to go, people to see.
• Ask questions you can't answer.
• Write a letter.
• Try to sneak a quarter into somebody's belongings.
• Draw something you see from where you're sitting.
• Pretend you're from another planet. (Skip this if you are.)

• Think of something nice to do for somebody. Now do it.

Above all, if you're bored don't whine about it. For one thing, you leave yourself wide open for a lecture about how somebody doesn't have time to entertain you, and if you weren't so lazy . . . You know the rest.

It's a mistake to complain about being bored, because what goes on in your head is your responsibility. You can't pass that off on anyone else; you probably don't want to anyway since that's how you got bored to begin with.

The solution to boredom is to take control of your own fun. If what's going on isn't good enough, find a way to make it better (without being obnoxious, please). When you do, you will have taken the party with you (which makes people want to be around you) and you'll become a leader (guaranteed).

BREAKING UP

This is one of the toughest things you'll ever have to do. Here are some ideas that might help just a little bit.

• Don't judge the quality of your relationship by one date, one weekend, or one week. It's how you do over the long haul that matters.

• Don't put it off. If your heart *has* changed, let your friend know. She has already sensed the change, anyway, and is only waiting for an explanation. Putting it off means lying, pretending, and feeling guilty because you are only *acting* like you care for someone as much as he *honestly* cares for you.

• Be straightforward. All the excuses for your change of heart won't make the news any easier. Sit down and talk it out.

• Accept responsibility yourself. Without being insincere, take as much of the blame for the breakup as you can. If you start heaping blame on your girlfriend, she may throw it back at you only in self-defense. A boyfriend is enough to lose in one day—don't make her lose face, too.

• Don't ever say *"just* friends"—the two words are contradictory (like *just* a unicorn, or *just* a billion dollars), and you degrade the concept of friendship by connecting them. (See Friendship.)

• If you break up, break up. Don't tease or confuse her by spending time with her when you're lonely or

when you don't have another date or when you need an ego boost. If these are the only times you miss the relationship, then breaking up was exactly what the two of you needed.

See: Dating, It's Getting Too Serious.

BULIMIA

See: Eating Disorders.

CHEATING

Cheating is when you interfere with the facts so that things come out in your favor. It's a form of stealing—you steal the truth and replace it with a lie that looks just like it. For example, when you cheat on a test, the stolen article is the C you would have gotten, and the lie is the A that took its place. When you cheat on your income tax, the stolen truth is the money you *actually* made last year; the lie is the amount you *say* you made.

The problem with cheating is that it's addicting—it's a thrill to rearrange reality until it suits your tastes. And the feeling that you're getting something for nothing is delightful, because you can remember so many times when you got nothing for working your tail off—"It's only fair to cheat; she gave me a C on the last test when I deserved an A." But if you cheat enough, trying to cope in life without rearranging the facts becomes a real chore. (And it doesn't take long—cheating is a strong drug.)

When you stop cheating in school, there's bad news and there's good news. The bad news is that unless you study harder, your grades are probably going to suffer. The good news is—so what? There still seems to be a place in this world for honest people, so don't worry that all of life's cherries will go to those who sneaked into the orchard. (And if *you* get there the honest way, you will ensure that there will still be a place by the time your children start looking.) Yes, cheaters *do* prosper—but so do honest people. Why sell out on your character just to save a little effort?

For ideas on getting through school the honest way, see Studying.

More: Philippians 4:8.

CHURCH

Churches are like families—under one roof the most wonderful and least wonderful things are likely to happen. You take the bad with the good.

Several images merge to define a church. One is the congregation: people gathering from a lot of different experiences to share an experience together. The congregation is a homey image, like a big family getting together for a happy Thanksgiving meal.

Another church image is the circle—the convergence of people to form something that wouldn't be there or wouldn't be the same if each were not in his place.

A third image of the church is the Body of Christ. As surely as God chose to enter human experience with a human body in Jesus Christ (that's what we call *incarnation*), he has chosen to be present in the world today through his people, the Body of Christ.

This is an amazing notion made believable only because it is so explicitly described in Scripture. God once again does the unexpected, declaring that the Church, in its weaknesses and failures, is the object of his pleasure and the point of his contact with the world. Outrageous! And true.

If you're ever looking for a church for yourself, consider these questions:

• What do you think are the privileges and responsibilities of belonging to the Church?
• What do you like best about your past church experience? What would you change? Why?
• There are a lot of churches that seem to be okay at first but have non-biblical ideas about the identity of Christ. Since Christ is what Christianity is all about, what does a prospective church say about him?
• If you have to give and take on things like travel distance, size, denomination, peer-group involvement, or worship style, what trade-offs are you willing to make?

More: Acts 2:42-47, 1 Corinthians 12:12-31, Ephesians 4:1-16, Hebrews 10:19-25.

COCAINE

What's all the fuss about coke? A friend of ours tried snorting some once and nearly drowned.

See: Alcohol, Crystal, Materialism, Steroids, Substance Abuse.

COMMITMENT

Commitment—making a choice and living with it to the end. It's not easy to be committed in a world that's dedicated to keeping its options open. But it's necessary.

People who are unwilling to commit themselves to ideas and ideals and to other people end up alone. It's that simple. Nobody really trusts someone who won't make a commitment when the chips are down.

Coaches look at commitment more than ability because—as they delight to tell us—when the going gets tough, the tough get going.

Employers look for commitment because the welfare of their business can hardly be entrusted to someone who calls in sick when he wants to go to a party.

Parents look for commitment because they're not about to give the keys of a $17,000, ton-and-a-half automobile to someone who won't take the trouble to call when she knows she'll be late.

Friends look for commitment because they can't afford to trust their hearts to someone who may bail out for a better offer.

God looks at commitment because *he* is committed and will give himself completely to people who give themselves completely to him.

You look for commitment in others, don't you?

See: Accountability, Friendship, Living Together, Marriage.

COMPASSION

When you see someone in pain and hurt for them so much you can't look away, that's compassion. Compassion is a remarkably demanding word that means *to suffer with*. When we see lonely, hungry, hurting people, Christ calls us to suffer with them. Matthew's Gospel tells us that when Jesus saw the crowds, "he had compassion on them, because they were harassed and helpless, like sheep without a shepherd." And then Jesus said an amazing thing to his disciples: "The harvest is plentiful but the workers are few. Ask the Lord of the harvest, there- fore, to send out workers into his harvest field."[1] And Jesus made his disciples into the very workers he asked them to pray for, all in response to compassion.

Who are the people in your world who seem harassed and helpless, like sheep without a shep- herd? Is there a way for you to share their suffering?

More: The Compassion Project, from Compassion International—films, tapes and discussions to help your youth group learn how to respond to the needs of the poor. Call 1-800-336-7676 for information. Also *Ideas for Social Action* (Youth Specialties/Zondervan, 1983) by Anthony Campolo contains hundreds of practical ideas for you and your friends.

[1]Matthew 9:36-38.

CREATIVITY

You may never be more like God than when you're creative—using old things in new ways, rearranging them like they've never been put together before. (This, of course, is a dim reflection of God, who makes something out of nothing!) Many people think creativity is inborn—you either have it or you don't. Here's what we think: first, creativity is possi- ble for everyone. It's a human trait as universal as thought and speech and small-muscle coordination. (Some people are better or faster, but almost every- one can perform well enough to get by.) Second, creativity is learned. You can exercise your creativity until it's healthy and strong.

Seven reasons to cultivate creativity:
• Creativity is fun!
• Creativity makes a difference in the world by finding answers to difficult questions.
• Creative people encourage others to try new ways of doing things.

• Acting creatively makes you feel alive!
• Creative people can afford to be generous. Walt Disney, for example, once calmed some anxious employees who were afraid outsiders would exploit Disney's ideas because he was so open with his

"secrets." He reassured them, "I can create faster than they can steal."
• People like to be around creative folks.

Five attitudes that kill creativity:
• "I'm not creative."
• "It's been tried before."
• "They wouldn't like it."
• "It's too expensive."
• "I might fail."

Eleven ideas for cultivating your own creativity:
• Hang out with creative people.
• Ask "What can I do that hasn't been done before?"
• Connect the five senses to whatever you're working on. What does it look like, smell like, feel like, taste like, sound like? Include sensory descriptions in an English paper. Design a science project around them.
• Consider what you've already done that you can recycle and make even better.
• Ask "What emotions, positive and negative, can I connect with the idea I'm working on?
• Ask "Would I do this the same way for someone else?"
• Try to do your work so well that other people will want to show it off.
• Pray like crazy!
• Take a beginning art class. Read *Drawing on the Right Side of the Brain* (Tarcher/Houghton Mifflin; 1979) by Betty Edwards, or another book that will help you learn to draw.
• Nurture friendships that will help you overcome the fear of failure.
• Keep trying until you get it right!
  See: Dreaming.

CRYSTAL

Crystal methamphetamine is one of a batch of "designer drugs" you can find in your town if you ask around. People buy crystal because it takes them

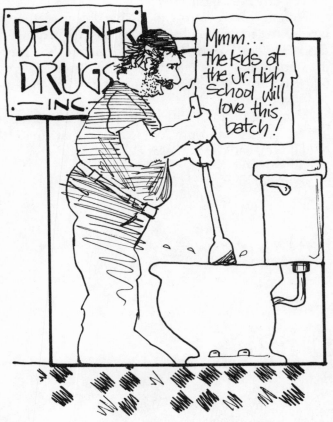

high—fast—for relatively little money. The downside of crystal (why does there always have to be a downside?) is that what goes up higher and faster comes down lower, faster, and longer. Downside effects include chronic dependency (that means "I need more and I need it *now*"), paranoia, confusion, panic, anxiety, hallucinations, sweating, crankiness, and depression. People who are coming down carry the effects for weeks, even months. The truth is, at this writing, nobody is quite sure how long crystal stays in the body nor all the effects.

Designer drugs are called that because they're compounded from other chemicals to produce a desired effect. We shudder to think about the experimentation that goes into developing drugs like crystal. Who are the guinea pigs? You can bet that the chemists aren't.

And what about quality control? This stuff is made in somebody's bathroom. Who knows what's in it? It's not like you can check the label.

Will we ever learn?

See: Addiction, 502, Help, Steroids.

DATE RAPE

See: Rape.

DATING

Three facts:

1. It's okay not to date. (Lots of people don't get into dating until college.)

2. Dates don't have to be romantic. (Romance has its place, but the best dates are fun and relationship-building.)

3. A date doesn't have to look like a date. (Any activity that lets you get to know one another better can be called a date—whether it's puddle jumping, grocery shopping, or a tour of a tennis-ball factory with ten of your friends.)

Cheap dating ideas: Go people-watching at the mall or airport. Have a picnic in the rain. Shop for ridiculous clothing at garage sales. Get friends and family to serve you a gourmet meal in your living room. Go to different grocery stores and test all the

39

sample foods. Roast marshmallows over the bar-
becue pit in a park.

More: Doug Fields and Todd Temple, *Creative Dating* and *More Creative Dating* (Thomas Nelson, 1986,
1987); Chap Clark, *Next Time I Fall in Love* (Youth
Specialties, 1987).

DEPRESSION

Almost everyone feels depressed from time to
time—disappointed, unmotivated, tired, helpless,

flat. We ride it out and, most of the time, the depression just goes away. We can't really say why it disappears any more than we can say for sure what brought it on.

But sometimes depression doesn't just go away; instead, it gets deeper, and the depressed person feels hopeless and isolated. Relationships suffer. Sleep becomes a hiding place or so disrupted that a whole night's slumber is only a memory. The behavior of a deeply depressed person may surprise even him: trouble at school, boredom, anger, defiance, restlessness, hell-raising, feelings of worthlessness, inability to have fun, avoidance and fear of ordinary tasks like homework and household chores, thoughts of suicide.

The truth is that lots of adolescents find themselves inexplicably in deep depression. It doesn't usually happen overnight. Parents hope that it's only a stage. Other adults conclude that the depressive behavior merely proves that kids are generally obnoxious. Friends may or may not understand and may or may not hang around to see what happens.

Adolescence is tough no matter what. When you add depression to the package, a person can feel overwhelmed. Seventy percent of those who attempt suicide are or have been depressed.[1] So what can we do to help?

Watch for signs of depression in your friends. The symptoms listed above may indicate a friend in need of a friend.

Just listen to what your friends say. Playing junior psychologist may do more harm than good. A depressed friend needs an active, compassionate listener. Let her know she's not as isolated as she feels by lending your understanding ear.

Guide a depressed person to help. Severe depression puts a person at risk. That means that the chance of life-threatening behavior increases to the point that someone with experience should be included in your conversation. Take him to a youth worker, a trusted teacher, counselor, or administrator at school. If he's really depressed, he probably won't put up too much of a struggle.

If you're feeling depressed, there are a couple of things you can do:

• Take a hard look at the sources of your discouragement, and then take some significant action. If it's school, get help, reorganize your schedule, read a book, begin writing the paper—do *something*. If a broken relationship is the cause, write a letter, make a phone call, forgive, and take a healthy step towards resolving the conflict (some steps are *not* healthy, of course). If guilt is the problem, confess your fault and do what you can to make it right.

• Find someone to talk to. There's no shame in feeling depressed—unless there's shame in being human. You don't have to—shouldn't, in fact—go through depression alone.

See: Compassion, Friendship, Help, Listening, Loneliness, Suicide, When You Don't Know What To Say.

[1]Brent Q. Hafen and Kathryn J. Frandsen, *Youth Suicide: Depression and Loneliness* (Cordillera Press, 1986).

DIETING

See: Eating Disorders, Food, Losing Weight.

DIVORCE

What can you say about divorce? Nobody enters marriage planning on divorce, though a lot of folks seem to keep that option open, just in case.

Divorce feels like failure, like regret, like favorite recipes never tasted again, like intimacy gone forever. Divorce feels like death, and people mourn like crazy when they lose their mate.

Too bad about divorce. Everybody gets hurt. Even when splitting up solves some big problems—and sometimes it solves some whoppers—it also creates new ones. As Allie says to Kate, "You're married for eight or twelve years, but you're divorced for the rest of your life."

A lot of kids feel divorced, too. "When Dad left he didn't just leave Mom; he left me, too. I'm hurt and angry—I don't know if I can forgive him." That's a pretty common sentiment. Here's another one: "It's been about six years, and I just can't shake the feeling that if I'd been a better kid they'd still be together."

Feelings range from guilt to outrage, and most of us hold them inside as if we were alone. But we're not. Half the people you know live with only one biological parent. It's tough, but it's just the way things are.

Here are some things to think about if you're dealing with divorce:

• It's not much easier on your parents than it is on you. Their feelings are like raw meat. They don't need to be punished—they need to be loved.

• Forgiveness is costly *and* necessary. Don't act like it's no big deal. Look at the divorce as clearly as you can, add up the hurt and wrong, then talk with someone you trust about starting to forgive.

• You don't have to be in the dark about the split. It's okay to ask questions. Be as generous as you can when you ask, and respect your parents' right to say, "I can't answer that now; give me some time." Don't wait for them to tell you what you want to know—they may never get around to that on their own.

• Don't imagine you could have stopped the divorce, and don't suppose you can get them back together again. It wasn't your fault (no matter how guilty you may feel and no matter how much you may have been caught in the middle). The only thing that could bring them together again is an act of God to which *they* would have to be open. Consider it dead unless God performs a bona fide resurrection.

• You are responsible for what you do next. One kid put it this way: "It was dawn when my mom came into my bedroom. She had been up all night, and her eyes were red from crying. She sat on the edge of my bed and put her head on my chest and sobbed. I knew what was next. I could tell it was over. And I thought, 'I could do *anything* now and get away with it. People would just think, well, he's from a broken home.' But I knew I couldn't live with that. That was an important moment for me."

• What can you learn about yourself from this unhappiness? How do you feel about marriage? What sort of spouse do you want to be? What sort of parent do you want to be?

• Get help. It doesn't make sense to carry this unhappiness alone when there are so many people who can lend a hand.

More: The book of Hosea, Matthew 19:1-12.
See: Marriage, Parents, Stepparents.

DOUBT

"Doubt," said Frederick Buechner, "is the ants in the pants of faith. It keeps it alive and moving."[1] Some people think it's a sin to have doubts about God, but to doubt is just to admit wonder; to say, "I don't know everything and I wish I knew more." That's not a sin.

The sin is in not caring to know more about God — thinking you've got him all figured out and there's nothing he can do to surprise you. The person who thinks that *needs* to doubt, and what she ought to doubt most of all is herself.

Author Madeleine L'Engle (remember *A Wrinkle in Time*?) was once questioned by a friend who asked, "Now wait a minute; are you telling me you believe in God completely, without any doubts?"

"No," Ms. L'Engle replied, in measured tones. "I'm telling you I believe in God completely, with all kinds of doubts."

That's faith: to believe with everything you've got, in spite of the honest questions in your heart and mind, because you know and trust God — who doesn't lie.

So ask your questions right out loud. Expect God to hear them and, sooner or later, to answer them. When you obey God, all the while shaking your head and saying under your breath, "I can't believe you're asking me to do this," you're proving that you doubt your doubts as much as you doubt your faith. When you do that, an unwritten law says, your faith wins.

[1]Frederick Buechner, *Wishful Thinking* (Harper & Row, 1973).

THE DRAFT

Article I, Section 8 of the U.S. Constitution gives Congress the right "to provide for calling forth the Militia to execute the Laws of the Union, suppress Insurrections, and repel Invasions." The "militia" the Constitution refers to is made up of all able-bodied male citizens between eighteen and forty-five years old who aren't already members of the armed forces. The armed forces (Army, Navy, Air Force, Marines) usually have enough volunteers to cover all of their responsibilities, so the "calling forth," or draft, typically goes into effect only during wartime.

The U.S. is rare in the military service it requires of its citizens. In many countries *every* teenager, regardless of gender, must serve one year (and sometimes longer) in the military—war or no war. Others allow you to choose non-military work during your required period of service. But the freedom to do virtually anything you want when you graduate from high school is very rare.

Biblical cases have been built to defend the idea that Christians cannot obey Christ by joining the armed forces because to do so would condone violence.[1] But biblical cases have also been built to defend the position that Christians serve God by serving the government—a government God established in order to carry out his justice, punish evildoers, and protect the innocent.[2]

The argument has been going on for several hundred years, and there's much more to it than just this. If you want to find out more, ask your pastor for books or articles on the subject. Many denominations have prepared booklets that outline various opposing views in as simple a fashion as one can do with such a tough topic. See if you can track down one from your church to see what its views are.

If you're an eighteen-year-old guy, you're required by law to register at your local post office. If you don't register, the government will probably come looking for you. If you intend to take a stand on this issue by refusing to register, you had better take a long and serious look at the price you might pay for your belief. On the other hand, if you believe that register-ing is a compromise of your faith but you do so anyway, you will pay a price in other ways.

See: Nuclear War.

[1]See Matthew 5:38-48; Luke 6:27-36.
[2]See Romans 13:1-7.

DREAMING

Lots of people talk about the importance of dreams and what they mean. But the really important dreams are the ones you have when you're awake.

Awake-dreaming is when you imagine something that doesn't exist or hasn't happened. If what is in the world is the best it can be, then dreaming is a waste of time. But since you can take just about anything in this world and say, "What if . . . ?," you know that there's room for dreaming: "What *if* there was a cure for AIDS?" "What *if* there was a way for my friends and me to keep people from starving?" "What *if* there were fun parties in our community where you didn't have to drink to fit in?"

Dreaming gives you a taste of things that could be. If that taste is sweet, you'll go through all sorts of trouble to re-create that flavor so others can share in the pleasure.

You dream a lot when you're a child. The taste of better things keeps you going because you can't quite get the memory of that sweet "what if" out of your mind. The problem is that you see so much "what is" as you get older that you stop dreaming about "what if." If you manage somehow to keep on dreaming, people call you idealistic or impractical or a dreamer.

But if you read the stories of those who have made a difference in the world, you discover their common habits—they never stopped dreaming, and they never stopped trying to re-create their dreams in real life. Here are some tricks we use to keep ourselves dreaming:

• Read fairy tales, classic literature, children's stories, and fantasies. Your education probably already taught you all about what *is*; you also need to know about what *if*. In *The Voyage of the Dawn Treader* (the third book of the *Chronicles of Narnia*), author C.S. Lewis introduces Eustace Clarence Scrubb, a miserable boy who was "quite incapable of making anything up himself" because he had "read none of the right books."

• Read history (sorry about that) and biographies to find out how others took their dreams and applied them to real life. This can also help you avoid dreaming the wrong things. For example, reading about leaders like Constantine and Hitler will save us all from dreams like "What *if* we established a Christian government?"

• Share your dreams with people you trust. They'll encourage you and maybe even join you in making your dream a reality. Creativity consultant Mike

Vance tells the story of two fifteen-year-old ambulance drivers in World War I. In the midst of their gruesome tasks, they began dreaming about what each would do if they owned their own companies—how they would treat employees, serve customers, and market their products. Idealistic teenage dreams? You bet. These two dreamers were Ray Kroc (the creator of McDonald's restaurants) and Walt Disney.

• Ask God for wisdom as you pursue your dreams. Glorify him in what you do. Psalm 37:4 says, "Delight

yourself in the Lord and he will give you the desires of your heart."

See: Creativity.

DRUGS

See: Substance Abuse.

EATING DISORDERS

Sally felt concerned for the two girls she heard vomiting—what were the chances of *two* people being sick at the same time, in side-by-side toilets? But they emerged from the end stalls, McDonald's cups in hand, not looking a bit the worse for their retching. They weren't sick at all, but just taking a moment to toss their lunch before fifth period. Sally, on the other hand, began feeling a little queasy.

A 1984 survey of girls in an affluent San Diego public high school revealed that nineteen percent engaged in bulimic behavior.[1] And a 1986 Stanford

University Medical School survey of 1,728 high-school sophomores found that one in eight had attempted to control body weight by vomiting or taking drugs of some sort.[2] The Stanford study, by the way, marks the first time that boys made a significant numerical showing.

Bulimia is binge eating (eating way too much—like 2,000 calories in a half-hour), then purging (getting rid of the food by vomiting or taking a laxative or diuretic). The bulimic is aware that her pattern is abnormal, afraid she may not be able to stop, and depressed after binges. Because bulimics go on crash diets, their weight may fluctuate wildly. Bulimic behavior is generally learned, directly or indirectly, from other bulimics.

The reaction of many people to bulimia is, "Gross! Why would anybody do that?" (People occasionally eat more than they intend and go to bed with a stomachache, but most don't solve the problem by vomiting.)

Then there's the other end of eating disorders—anorexia. Anorexia nervosa is a psychosomatic disorder (that means it's a mental-emotional response with physical symptoms). The anorexic girl (only a small percentage of anorexics are boys) responds to personal problems by starving herself. She is likely to have a distorted body image, thinking she is thirty percent or forty percent larger than she is. She lives with a fear of obesity that doesn't go away when she loses weight. It isn't that she's not interested in food—she may be preoccupied with food preparation and may own a library of cookbooks. It's just that she does not or cannot eat. Psychiatrists speculate that anorexic behavior may be triggered when someone tells a girl she is fat, she has a bad sexual experience, or is threatened by the separation of her parents.

People with eating disorders are genuinely suffering. Even if you argue that she brought it on herself—a point you'd be hard-pressed to prove—if you spend a little time with someone who is struggling with anorexia or bulimia, you'll know she is in real pain.

Like anyone in pain, she needs compassion and friendship.

If you're struggling with an eating disorder, please get help now. You can talk with your doctor, who will know immediately what questions to ask and how to help. Or you might confide in your mother. If it's been going on for any length of time, she may already suspect something. A youth worker or some other trusted adult can help you look for help. If you can't find another source, try Overeaters Anonymous. They can tell you who to call. Don't carry this problem alone and don't wait. It's dangerous—even deadly.

See: Compassion, Friendship, Losing Weight, Private Parts.

[1]Much of this material came from a seminar by Dr. James M. Ferguson at San Luis Rey Hospital, Encinitas, California.

[2]Study by Joel D. Killen reported in the magazine *Focus on the Family*, July 1986.

EMBARRASSMENT

Embarrassment is one of those things that's there to remind us that, no matter how enlightened, good looking, or powerful we humans think we are, each of us is still capable of something outrageously stupid at any moment. Embarrassment isn't the feeling you get when you do something stupid. (You probably don't even notice half of the dumb things you do.) Nor is it when other people see you do something stupid. Embarrassment is the feeling you get when you *realize* you've done something stupid and you *think* others saw you do it.

Three facts about embarrassment:

Fact one. Not as many people saw you walk into that wall as you think. Don't worry. Of the fifty people you think saw you, there were really only seven—and two of them were busy bumping into each other,

another three were picking up a fourth who had tripped on her shoelace, and the last person was scraping dog doo off his shoe.

Fact two. Even if people did notice, you've given them the opportunity to laugh. Have you ever been depressed or in a bad mood and then were knocked out of it by a good fit of laughter? Feel good knowing that you may have just done that for someone else. And if a member of your audience needed a self-image boost, he got it because you reminded him that he is not the only less-than-perfect soul alive. By the way, you can laugh too. Just try to imagine what you must have looked like, and let the laughter roll.

Fact three. If you lean against a wet counter top in the rest room and soil your trousers in exactly the wrong place, you are in for some embarrassment unless you do one of two things: either splash water all over yourself to make it look like the faucet exploded, or immerse your pants in a full sink of water to make them uniformly dark.

See: The Imaginary Audience.

ENGAGEMENT

See: Living Together, Marriage.

FAIRNESS

See: Justice.

FAITH

See: Doubt, Monday Morning.

FATHER

See: Parents.

FIGHTING

See: Arguing.

502

You're standing around a smashed car that the Highway Patrol brought over to school for Students Against Driving Drunk. It's a 502, a driving-under-the-influence, and it's pretty grim. Everything is where it landed after the accident: books on the floor in the back; a tampon on the dashboard, thrown there out of an open purse. A circle in the windshield on the passenger side is smashed like a spider web and pushed outward in the rough shape of a forehead. Tufts of curly hair are stuck in the spider web where the shatterproof glass spread on impact and then closed again before the passenger's head snapped back.

Nobody is talking much. As people wander by, they talk very quietly, like at a funeral. Then a girl says, "When I see something like this I swear I'll never drink and drive again . . . " and her voice trails off, like there's more she's going to say.

So you say, "And . . . "

"And . . . I probably will," she says. You can hardly believe it.

You doubt it's the right thing to say, but you go with your emotions: "Yeah, well, if you hurt somebody, I want you to know that we'll find you and we'll look you in the eye and call you a murderer." Now she's the one who can't believe it.

You just stand there, feeling awkward until she wanders off with that "What's your problem?" look on her face. But she doesn't say it, because she knows it's her problem.

And yours.

Candy Lightner, the woman who founded Mothers Against Drunk Drivers after her daughter was killed in a 502, said: "Don't call it an accident. If you drink and drive, it's no accident."

Through the mid-eighties there have been close to 100,000 alcohol-related deaths *per year*. That's 100,000 people with curly hair, books on the back seat, and somebody waiting at home. Put another way, that's almost twice as many Americans dead each year as were killed during *ten* years of involvement in Vietnam.

Where's the sense in that?

More: Ephesians 5:15-21, especially verse 18.

FREEDOM

Turning eighteen sounds like the first day of a new life, like freedom herself singing loud and late into the night. Turning eighteen is the hope of unbridled personal expression. "I can't wait till I turn eighteen . . . Things will be different when I'm eighteen."

Turning eighteen is one of life's great promises.

It is also one of life's unkept promises.

Ask around. There is no such thing as absolute freedom. Everybody works for somebody. The richest guy in the world pays somebody to tell him when to get up and when to be in Paris for his meeting with the president. If you think that freedom means doing whatever you want to do, think again.

On the other hand, freedom isn't just a phantom. Freedom means being responsible for yourself, and you don't have to wait till you're eighteen for that. You can nurture all kinds of freedom by taking responsibility for the details of your life. If you want freedom, sweat out the details. Keep your room in order, come in when you say you will or call if you're going to be late, put gas in the car, work ahead on your homework, save ten percent of your allowance or paycheck, respect your family and friends, keep your word. Your parents will give you freedom when they learn to trust you. If they're reasonably intelligent, that shouldn't take too long.

See: Accountability.

FRIDAY NIGHT

This is the night that half the teenage population sits at home wishing they were having as much fun as the other half are pretending to have.

Whichever half you relate to the most, here are some ideas you and a few friends can use to make Friday night (or any other night) an event:

• Hold a car rally. Team up a few friends in each car and send them out on a hunt for answers to the clues listed on a sheet. Or send out each car with a Polaroid camera and a list of photos to take.

• Have a progressive dinner by going to each other's houses to eat the leftovers from your parents' meals.
• Have a late-night picnic at the park or beach.
• Play broom hockey in a lit parking lot (or wait for a full moon).
• Borrow a video camera and make your own movie. Or interview people as they leave a theater to get their reactions to the movie.
• Go as a group to your friends' houses (preferably those who aren't home at the time). Bring along a camera and ask the parents if you can take pictures of your friends' bedrooms. Vote on the cleanest, messiest, best looking. Show the photos around at school.
• Have a cookie-baking marathon.
• Write letters and postcards to a friend who has just moved. See if you can get fifty pieces of mail written in one evening—then mail them all.
• Create and produce a date night for your parents. Have you and your friends act as chauffeurs, doormen, waitresses, and chefs; serve an appetizer on the steps of city hall, then dinner in your garage and dessert on the roof. If the evening is a success, repeat the show for your friends' parents on the following weekends.
   See: Parties.

FRIENDSHIP

When you call somebody your friend, you're saying much more than, "I like you." You're making a commitment to love him and look out for his best interests. You're saying, "I'm at your service."

If you're a true friend, you'll deliver your service best not by giving him what he *wants,* but by trying to give him what he *needs.* That means occasionally doing things he may not enjoy—like telling him to stop a self-destructive habit. It means asking him tough questions when he pretends to have all the answers, and it also means hurting him with the truth when he starts to live a lie.

It's been said that an enemy is someone who stabs you in the back. If that's true, then a friend is someone who stabs you in the *front.* Friendship means holding your friend accountable, which is so important to a relationship that it has its own section in this book (Accountability).

There are other responsibilities you must take on if you want to call someone a friend. Here are a few:

Encouragement. It's a tough world, made tougher because you can do ninety-nine good things in a day that go unnoticed, yet get yelled at for walking into class 2.9 seconds after the tardy bell. Which is why your friend needs a cheerleader, an encourager who is there to catch him in the act of doing something good and pat him on the back for it. "Pleasant words are a honeycomb," is how Proverbs 16:24 puts it, "sweet to the soul and healing to the bones." Unless you are first an encourager, you have no right to call yourself a friend.

Confrontation. This is the uncomfortable job of letting your friend know that you disagree with the way he's behaving. It's one of the toughest and most loving things you can do. But don't confront him unless you're sure that (a) you're doing it because you love him, not out of spite, jealousy, or because you think you're better than him; (b) you've been an encourager to him; and (c) you're willing to hang in with him no matter what. Tell him that you love him and that it hurts you to see him doing what he's doing. Also tell him what you think the consequences will be if he continues acting that way.

Intervention. You may confront a friend over and over, but he fails to turn around. His behavior is destructive, and you're gravely concerned for him. If your friend is on a collision course with disaster, love dictates that you do whatever you can to divert the path. When you intervene, you team up with several others who care about your friend and set up a group confrontation. All of the guidelines of confrontation apply, but the message is so much more powerful when your friend is sitting down, surrounded by people who aren't afraid to love him enough to tell him he's messing up.

More: Galatians 6:2; *The Friendship Factor* (Augsburg Publishing, 1979), by Alan Loy.

GAY

See: Homosexuality.

GIVING AWAY YOUR FAITH

According to C.S. Lewis, the Christian faith is a lot like a disease that's healthy to catch. The problem is that you can't catch it on your own—you have to be exposed to the virus by a carrier, someone who already has the disease. Christians have tried all sorts of ways to infect others—TV, radio, books (*this* book contains the virus, for example), and even smacking people over the head — but nothing works nearly as well as personal contact. If you know some people you'd like to infect, spend lots of time with them. Even those who have strong defense systems can eventually lower them when they see the kind of person this disease is turning you into.

GOD

See: Abba, Jesus, Yahweh.

GOING OUT

See: Dating.

GOSSIP

A ventriloquist can make his words come out of somebody else's mouth.

A lip-sync performer can make someone else's words come out of his own mouth.

A gossip does both.

Gossip is one of an arsenal of weapons you can shoot with your mouth, including slander, defamation, and malicious talk. Gossip is the easiest of these to launch accidentally — it looks a lot like harmless conversation. Here's a test you can use to help you identify it. If you can't honestly answer yes to at least one of these questions, then you've got a weapon on your tongue.

1. Would you say what you're about to say if the person you're talking about were standing next to you?

ERNIE WAS AN EXPERT AT SHOOTING OFF HIS MOUTH!

2. Did the person you're talking about give you specific permission to say what you're about to say?

3. Are you sharing the information with your "secret listener?" This is someone very trustworthy who would *never* take the information beyond the two of you. He is there to listen, to encourage, and to advise you when necessary. For some, this is a spouse, a longtime friend, a counselor, or a minister. (If the person you're talking about has expressly asked you to share the information with *no one else*, this is not an option.)

More: Proverbs 11:13; James 3:3-12.

GPA

Did you hear about the guy who won the national Academic Decathlon in 1987? Won it hands down— beat the best high-school minds in America.

The kid was a C student.

A college freshman came home shocked at the end of his first semester at an Ivy League school — it seems he was offered big dollars to take a test for somebody else. Nosing around a bit, he found out that's not uncommon. In a large class the professor never gets names and faces together, never checks handwriting, never knows who's taking tests for whom. You can't get *into* that school without a strong GPA, but apparently you can get *out* of it without an education.

Your grade-point average is the numerical average of all your grades over a given period of time. Some people think your GPA is the most important thing about you.

It's not. For one thing, some people take classes that will increase their GPA but not necessarily their knowledge. The irony here is that some folks qualify for admission to a tough-to-get-into college not because they're educated, but because they've got a hot GPA. Combine that with a good SAT score (which indicates only an ability to take tests well), and *voilá*! You're in.

But a wise admissions policy looks at much more than test scores and GPA, and so should you. A good education is training in how to think well. Seventeenth-century teacher Thomas Trahern wrote, "As nothing is easier than to think, so nothing is more difficult than to think well." You betcha.

The trouble with much of modern education is that it fails to teach us to think—we don't learn how to learn. In ten years no one will care what your GPA is or was. Employers don't care what you *did*; they want to know what you can *do*. The future belongs to people who are lifelong learners.

A lot of students are asking the wrong question: "What kind of college will accept me?" The right question is more like "What kind of school is acceptable to me?"

And a word from Judy Grear, a teacher in Encinitas, California: "Sometimes it's more important to make good people than good students."

HELP

There's nothing wrong with needing help. Everybody needs it, and we all need it many times throughout our lives.

When you need it the most, you're usually in the worst condition to determine where to find it. By finding someone you can trust to help you look, you're more likely to get the help you need. Try talking to an older brother or sister, parent, youth worker, church worker, school counselor, teacher, or peer counselor at school. One of the roles of your youth minister (or priest, youth director, or whatever you call him or her) is that of a shepherd, which means when a sheep (that's you) goes astray (needs help), it's okay to bleat out (make a phone call) to the shepherd. The shepherd's job is to help you get back into safe territory. Don't be afraid to ask him or her for help.

When you do need help, your worst enemy is pride. Something inside you says it's wrong to admit that you're troubled, weak, or confused: "Everybody else seems to get along fine without help. What's so wrong with me that I can't make it on my own?"

If you hear yourself saying that, we've got news for you—you're not the only good actor out there. Most of us are able to display composure and bliss on the outside while falling apart on the inside. You'll be surprised how fast the costumes drop when you go to a fellow actor you trust and let him see your real character. Opening up not only helps you; it helps the other person. And it allows both of you to do what the Bible commands of us when it says, "Carry each other's burdens, and in this way you will fulfill the law of Christ." Find someone with big arms, and share your load.

See: Accountability, Friendship.

HOMOSEXUALITY

There's a world of difference between feelings and behavior. Just because you find yourself attracted to members of the same sex doesn't mean you're a homosexual. If what runs across our minds makes us instantly guilty of the act, then sooner or later we will all be thieves and murderers. What you do with your thoughts—mentally and physically—is what matters.

When homosexuality is mentioned in the Bible, it seldom stands alone. It's usually one of a list of behaviors that God doesn't want us messing with—adultery, fornication, idolatry, prostitution, drunkenness, slander, and theft, among others. While not all these sins are equal in popularity, consequences, or social acceptance, they are all selfish, rebellious, and punishable by death according to God's absolute judgment. That puts *all* of us on our death beds, *all* of us looking for a miraculous cure.

If you have struggled with homosexual behavior, welcome to the infirmary. Jesus said, "It is not the healthy who need a doctor, but the sick. I have not come to call the righteous, but sinners."[1] When you know there's something wrong with you, you pay attention to what the doctor says. Here's what the Doctor says:

Confess. God already knows what you've done, but admitting it to him is part of his way of forgiving you. "If we confess our sins," the Bible says, "he is faithful and just and will forgive us our sins and purify us from all unrighteousness."[2]

Find support. If you feel this is an area of temptation, it may be time to seek support from another person. Carefully seek out a Christian you can trust, then ask for his help. Consider talking to a minister or a Christian counselor.

If you *don't* struggle with homosexuality, then lighten up on the people who do. There's a million miles between hating homosexual behavior and hating homosexuals. Let's stop condemning people in the name of Jesus and sending them running from the only One who loves them enough to die for them.

[1]Mark 2:17.
[2]1 John 1:9.

HOPE

People who run away or gradually self-destruct or suddenly end their lives have one thing in common—they feel hopeless. Not just discouraged, but convinced that nothing will end their monotonous, aching pain.

By contrast, the faintest glimmer of hope that things could get better may keep a girl in a lousy romance, may give a boy the courage to forgive another beating from his alcoholic father, may embolden a disheartened teacher to face an insolent class one more morning.

Hope is the battery that jump-starts the human heart. As long as there's hope, we can keep going, keep trying, keep hoping—because hope reproduces hope.

All this is by design, and though we sometimes hope for the wrong things—that we'll be able to make it on our own, that we can wish a thing undone— hope is what draws us to God. The Apostle Paul talked a lot about hope, declaring that hope will not disappoint us because God is faithful. When all hell breaks loose on us, he says, "we know that in all things God works for the good of those who love him," and "if God is for us, who can be against us?"[1] That's hope—the expectation that there's nothing God can't turn into a miracle of deliverance and help.

What's bothering you right now? Is it bigger than you? Is it bigger than God?

[1]Romans 8:28, 31.

THE IMAGINARY AUDIENCE

You've seen them walking across the front of the gym, struttin' their stuff, sure that the whole school is watching their promenade instead of the basketball game. They are playing to the Imaginary Audience.

The other side of that is the uncomfortable feeling that everybody was watching when you closed your skirt in the car door, or the time your mother got out of the car at school to kiss you goodbye. That "everybody's watching" feeling is what psychologists call the Imaginary Audience.

People do interesting things in response to this audience. It may be the biggest factor in deciding that you've outgrown the goodbye hug or the kiss from your parents, and it certainly contributes to fashion statements. Whether you dress like everyone else or are an outrageous nonconformist, your choice of dress is probably based on the conviction that everybody is watching.

There's nothing at all wrong with this unless the Imaginary Audience causes us to do something we don't want to do—or *not do* something we *want* to do or *should* do. When we respond to pressure that's not really there, we've given control of our behavior to an audience that doesn't really exist.

The truth is, except for rare occasions and accidents, *nobody* is watching you. We know that's true because everybody else is watching to see if everybody else is watching them. It's all a self-centered mess. You could eat your clothes and wear your lunch and most of the people in the room wouldn't notice or care.

That's what the Imaginary Audience is about. It's wondering if anyone cares: "Am I okay? Do other people think I'm okay?"

Well, listen up! You're okay. Jesus cares enough about you to identify with you as completely as the infinite God can identify with someone he made. The writer of Hebrews says that God didn't give even angels the honor he gave you; that he isn't ashamed to call you his brother or sister.[1] He may be as invisible to you as your Imaginary Audience but, unlike it, he really is watching, with love in his eyes and a lot of pride.

More: Psalm 139:1-18; Matthew 6:25-34.

See: Embarrassment.

[1]Hebrews 2:15-18.

JESUS

Jesus is God's way of saying "Yes!"

God created everything out of nothing, did it perfectly, and did it at his discretion. The far-flung galaxies dance in a great rhythm that God began because he wanted to. Nothing landed out of place when he spoke the world into being—not a flash of light, not a moment of time, not a speck of earth. Everything was perfect.

And he looked at it all so fondly and said, "Good!" And he looked at humankind, like looking in a mirror of sorts, and said, "Real good!"

And they all lived happily for about as long as it took for the humans to turn real good into real bad. Yet even then things weren't as bad as they could be. But when God looked at humankind again, the mirror was broken.

Some folks claim that the flaw in the whole system was God's big mistake in giving them (and, I suppose, us) a choice. But that was no fault. It was love.

God showed just what sort of person he is by entering creation through the broken glass and shattered image of the mirror. He became one of us! What a miracle—God becoming a squirming, crying, drooling, wetting, squalling baby boy! While King

Herod had armed guards watching the front gate for uninvited guests, the real King of the Jews slipped unnoticed through the servants' entrance. Who could believe it?

God mended the broken image, made the glass shine like new, and he did it by becoming one of us— not less, not more, but completely human.

In Jesus Christ, God said, "Yes!" to the original plan, the only plan. Everything that went from good to bad got a brand new start in Jesus, and it's not because he *had* to do it. God *chose* to make the image right again because he wanted to, and he proved that the deed was done by the greatest feat of self-control creation has ever witnessed: "He made him who had no sin to be sin for us, so that in him we might become the righteousness of God."[1]

Then he sealed the deal by raising the One who became sin for us right out of the grave forever, period.

What it means for you to "become the righteousness of God" has something to do with what it means to say "Yes!" to God.

More: If you haven't read it (or haven't read it lately), look at the whole Gospel of Mark; Luke chapter 2; John chapter 1; Colossians 1:9-20; Philippians 2:5-11; Hebrews 1:1-2:18.

[1]2 Corinthians 5:21.

JOBS

How to find one:

If employers have a choice, they'll hire someone they know—or someone who knows someone they know—before hiring a complete stranger. That means the best way to look for a job is not in the want ads, but among your family and friends.

Ask your parents if they have any friends who own businesses or can somehow help you find a job where they work.

Ask your own friends about open positions where they work. If your friend is a good worker, his recommendation is worth a lot (and if he's a sloth, you may be getting *his* position).

If you strike out with your friendship connections,

don't get discouraged — you don't have to search the ads *yet*. Because most high-school and college students keep a job for less than a year, employers are constantly looking for new workers. Go to a place where you would like to work (dressed sharp), and ask the manager if there are any positions available. If there are no openings, ask if you can fill out an application anyway. Don't fill it out right there — take it home and bring it back later. Fill it out as neatly as you possibly can (type it if you have bad writing — no kidding), and staple a good photo to it (faces are easier to remember than names). When you take back the application, you will be showing that you are a reliable person, doing exactly what you said you would do, and that you want the job bad enough to go through all of this trouble. It also gives you an excuse to show your face one more time. Ironically, many employers won't take a second look at that application. The brief glance they give you and the application is all they may use to determine if you're the one for the job.

Since lots of workers don't give the boss much warning when they decide to quit, employers don't have lots of time to hunt through a stack of applications to track down a replacement. That's why it's so important to drop in again a week or two later to show your face to that potential boss. Give your name again, and ask if there is any news on an opening. It's awkward to do this, so give yourself an excuse: go in and buy something, and say, "By the way . . . ". Or type up a one-page resume and ask, "I put this together and thought it might help someone sorting through applications. Could you attach it to mine?" Or, if you can say it honestly, "My little brother sometimes forgets to take a message, and I thought there might be a slim chance you tried to call me."

Most likely, they'll be impressed with your interest, and if someone quit on that day, you may be in the right place at the right time. If there isn't a job for you, they'll still know you better than any other applicant—and they don't like hiring strangers, anyway.

How to keep one:

Your job is one of the toughest proving grounds for your faith. Behavior that's clearly wrong at home or among friends is standard conduct at the workplace. Work is where many people who disapprove of lying, cheating, and stealing have no problem calling in sick when they aren't, stretching the hours on their time card, or taking home supposedly free merchandise. If you want to keep your job, behave according to your faith, not according to the code of ethics that you see other workers following.

Imagine this: a friend has just told you that she thinks your job is ridiculous, boring, and pointless. To prove it, she's going to send spies to observe and record your work behavior for the next month. To support her claim, she's going to produce evidence: how you treat customers, the way you act toward fellow workers, the expression on your face, the amount of effort you put forth, and how you handle problems.

Your goal is to prove her absolutely wrong. For the next month no one is going to catch you doing anything but pushing your job to the limit—enjoying it more and doing it better than anyone ever could. Every moment you're on the job you're asking, "How can I do this task better? How can I make this person's day? What new skill can I develop that will increase my effectiveness? How can I learn from this mistake so that making it wasn't a complete waste?" By the time she's finished gathering evidence, she'll have no choice but to conclude that your job is the best one in the world. And at the end of this one-month "trial," you'll have convinced yourself that satisfaction in *any* job is nine-tenths attitude, and that your present attitude has turned *this* job into a thrilling and worthwhile adventure.

When to quit one:

A job can be a great thing to have, but it can also be the last thing you need right now. If you work a lot of hours, chances are your education is going to suffer. And so might your relationships. Like any demand on your time, there's going to be a trade-off. Ask yourself—does the pressure, conflicts, less time for studying, friendships, family, and other activities outweigh the benefits of the money and experience? The money you earn from a job can be used to buy clothes, records, and fun toys, yet those things will always be available. Earning that money can cost you time with your friends, family, and church—and all the wages in the world won't be enough to buy that time back.

Other reasons to quit: you have an irresolvable conflict with a boss or co-worker; you're forced to work under unsafe conditions; you or your employer is doing something you believe to be immoral or illegal; others are having a negative influence on your behavior or attitude; you're being sexually or physically harassed; you've found a job that will be better for you.

Whatever your main reason is, carefully write out all of the positives and negatives of the job, and save the list. Next time you look for a job, review the list: that way you can avoid getting yourself into a similar situation.

How to quit one:

If you're a bad worker, your boss may be so excited about being saved from the trouble of firing you that he won't even bother to ask for a reason. But if you've been a good worker, he's likely to demand a reason for your decision to quit. Know your honest reason before he asks, or else you might get talked into staying, you might start an argument, or you might even make an enemy. If it's the money, tell him—but be ready for the possibility that he'll offer you more.

If you've found a better job, tell him you think you would be happier at it. If the reason why the new job is better is beyond his control (e.g., closer to home, related to your career interests, better hours), let him know so he won't feel personally responsible. If he *is* the reason why you're leaving, it's usually best not to say it in so many words (unless you have a very good relationship with him, and you think that he would want to know). Tell him the other job will work better for you—and if he digs for deeper reasons, mention one or two of the secondary reasons you have for making the switch. Arguing about his weaknesses is not your responsibility, and you could jeopardize a good recommendation and cause him to take out his anger on other employees, especially those he knows are your friends. If your reason for quitting is to spend more time with family, friends, school, or church, tell him.

When you give your the boss the news, let him have two weeks' notice to give him time to find a replacement. But just because you give him that much time, it doesn't mean he has to give *you* that much. He may find it more convenient to have you go immediately—like if someone just came in that day looking for a job. He also may keep you on until you start *acting* like you're leaving, working with an "I don't care anymore" attitude. If you want to work for the next two weeks—and get a good recommendation for your next job—you're going to have to work your tail off.

JUSTICE

Justice is the principle you appeal to when you cry, "That's not fair!" Based on the number of times you hear that phrase repeated, it's clear that most of us are keenly aware of the concept, at least as it applies to what's fair—and what isn't—about the treatment we receive from others. "That's not fair—*I* didn't do it! *I* don't deserve it! *I* am entitled to it!" The justice we appeal to is a *me* justice—something is *just* if it's just for me. But there is another kind of justice.

The Bible talks about justice a lot, usually referring to it as something you *do*—not something you receive. It's not something you demand for yourself as much as something you do on behalf of others. Micah 6:8 is a short list of what God requires of us: to act justly, love mercy, and walk humbly with God. Justice seems like one of God's favorite inventions. If you want to take this Scripture to heart, then start fighting injustice.

To fight it, you've got to find it. The first place to look is inside yourself. Do you treat others with justice? If you're a supervisor on a job or have leadership responsibilities at church, club, or school, injustice is your worst enemy. In such places it often travels under other names like favoritism, back-stabbing, kissing up, partiality, and gratuities.

The second place to look is around you. If you have a good sense of *me* justice, put yourself in another person's shoes and see if you feel like crying, "That's not fair!" If so, then you can bet he's a victim of injustice. Maybe you see a girl back her car into another car and then take off without leaving a note. Or maybe you hear your friends ridicule someone because he has a foreign accent. Or someone is accused of something you know she didn't do. Unfortunately, finding injustice isn't hard.

What's worse? *Fighting* it. The classic symbol of justice is a scale; fighting injustice means balancing that scale. To act justly, you've got to see that the wrong is righted, that the imbalance is corrected. That could cost you time, money, and relationships.

One last thought. Don't confuse *just* with *legal*. Laws attempt to maintain justice and prevent injustice, but on occasion they do the reverse—preventing justice and maintaining injustice. As of this writing, the twenty-six million black people of South Africa are forbidden by law to vote, thus making justice for blacks illegal. And here in the U.S. it's legal for a woman to end the life of her unborn son if she desires to have a girl instead—making injustice against unborn children legal. In the unfortunate instances when you have to choose between the two, remember that God's command is to act justly.

More: Leviticus 19:15; Proverbs 16:11; 17:15; 18:5; 24:23-26; Zechariah 7:9-10.

Kissing

Kissing is a lot of fun.

The more you kiss someone, the more you want to do other things that seem even more fun. The trouble is when you start doing the things that seem even *more* fun, you can get yourself into a situation that isn't fun.

The Bible doesn't really say too much about things like kissing, but it does have a lot to say about the things that kissing leads to.

• Long periods of kissing (like an hour or longer) is tough on the lips—and tough on the willpower. After you've kissed your brains out for an hour, you start hearing little voices saying, "Hey, my hands are getting bored. My mouth is having all the fun. Hmm. I wonder what I could do with my hands to keep from getting bored. I know—I think my hands can do a little investigating." Our experience indicates that the investigating your hands do is usually not in the knee area.

• Uh, how do we say this? When your kissing moves to the trading-bubble-gum-saliva-transfer-passionate-tongue stage, you're in trouble.

• Unfortunately, because of the times we live in, kissing is becoming more and more dangerous to your health (you know, herpes and all that stuff). Another thing—when you *start* your kissing with the French open-mouth technique, it really cheapens a kiss. When you are particular about who you kiss and how you kiss, it is amazing what happens: your kiss actually becomes special. It actually means something.

A kiss is meant to be special. It is supposed to be a means of communicating with someone you care about very much. And when you are careful about your kissing, you can rediscover the many, many things you can communicate with your kissing. You can communicate friendship, appreciation, affection, love, empathy, and many other things. Most couples today see kissing as a necessary warm-up for the big-time stuff. The truth is that kissing can *be* the big-time stuff.

LEADERSHIP

See: Servanthood.

LISTENING

Have you noticed there's more talking going on than listening? It must be that a lot of us are talking to ourselves. Hardly seems right inasmuch as God gave us two ears and only one mouth. Still, kids, parents, siblings, friends, teachers, pastors—*everybody* looks like one of those guys you see in big cities, the ones who sit at the bus stops having earnest, loud conversations with nobody.

If you want to convince someone that he is unimportant, interrupt him before he's finished talking.

To persuade someone that it's pointless trying to talk to you—and insult her, to boot—ignore what she says.

People will believe you're a know-it-all if, instead of listening to what someone is telling you, you think ahead to what you're going to say next.

If you want to scare someone into wondering if they really know you, cross your arms, stare into space, and clam up when they try to talk with you.

Roll your eyes a lot if you want someone to believe that you think what she says is stupid.

To convince a person you hate him, narrow your eyes, tighten your jaw, and stare right through him.

If you want to convince someone you care, listen.

If you want someone to teach you something, ask a question for which you don't know the answer—then listen.

To convince a person that she matters, look at her when she speaks.

Don't try mind reading if you want to find out what a person really thinks.

If you want someone to listen to *you*, keep your mouth shut until he's finished talking.

"Everyone should be quick to listen, slow to speak, and slow to become angry," says the Apostle in James 1:19.

LIVING FOREVER

"Someone once asked me if my dream was to live on in the hearts of my people, and I said I would like to live on in my apartment." (Woody Allen)

"I tell you the truth, whoever hears my word and believes him who sent me has eternal life and will not be condemned; he has crossed over from death to life." (Jesus, in John 5:24)

"And this is the testimony: God has given us eternal life, and this life is in his Son. He who has the Son has life; he who does not have the Son of God does not have life." (the Apostle John, in 1 John 5:11-12)

"I'll be with Jesus, and I won't be retarded anymore." (Jerry, a severely handicapped 35-year-old man).

LIVING TOGETHER

To be honest, there sure seems to be a lot of wisdom in it.

"It's better to try out the relationship before making a commitment of marriage."

"It gives you an opportunity to test your compatibility."

"It takes the pressure off the marriage by allowing you to enter into it gradually."

"If it doesn't work out, you can break up without the mess of a divorce."

"It's marriage without the legal certificate – and the expense of a wedding."

The Bible doesn't have as much to say on the topic. Except a few remarks like this:

"Flee from sexual immorality."[1]

Although this doesn't seem as convincing as the reasons *for* living together, ponder this before you unpack your toothbrush: "For the wisdom of this world is foolishness in God's sight."[2] And when you must choose between what seems right and what the Creator of the universe believes on the topic, go with the Creator.

See: Commitment.

[1] Corinthians 6:18.
[2] Corinthians 3:19.

LONELINESS

Loneliness may be the most common emotion of adolescence. People feel isolated, worthless, hollow, cut off from others who are feeling the same way.

In some ways, loneliness is a natural response to the storm of change that clouds adolescence. Every day the skies threaten and a lot of us go inside, waiting out the foul weather, hoping to stay dry.

But we're in this together! Why watch people turning up their collars against the winds of loneliness and not say, "Hey, I'm lonely too. Let's talk or go puddle-jumping or something."

This may be your chance to stand apart from the crowd in a small but very important way. It'll cost you something, but it's worth it to end the isolation for yourself and others. Just talk. It's so simple and yet so difficult. Talk to the people around you. Where is it written that you can't strike up a conversation with a stranger? That goes double when your opening line

can so easily be, "Weren't you in my English class last semester? What's your name?"

Some people may wonder about you at first, but so what—they already wonder about you. And very soon people will seek your company because you invited them in out of the rain to a warm friendship.

See: Adolescence, Friendship, Listening.

LOSING WEIGHT

Losing weight is an American obsession. It is, in fact, an industry in which billions of dollars are spent every year. The cultural assumption is that to be thin is everything.

Not so. A girl who panics because she can't fit into last year's bathing suit may have lost sight of the fact that her body has changed its shape—there are curves where the lines used to be, and curves take up more space. That's good news! That's growing up. The problem is that we are obsessed with a childish body image, an image no one can maintain and still remain healthy.

Yet there may be good reasons to lose weight, and if your health is at stake then you'd better find a way to do it.

The way to do it, of course, is self-control. In his book *The Fat Is in Your Head* (Word, 1984), Charlie Shedd admits that he's lost 1,500 pounds—the same twenty pounds over and over again. That's how it is with a lot of us. Weight comes and goes depending on the time of year and how we feel about ourselves. If you genuinely need to lose weight (and your doctor can tell you that), the answer is not purging or miracle diets or diuretics. The trick (if there is a trick) is the combination of smart, moderate eating and smart, moderate exercise. If your goal is health—and that ain't bad—then set some habits you can live with for a lifetime.

See: Eating Disorders.

MARRIAGE

Marriage is a happenin' deal. Really. No matter what your impression may be, the marriage of two people into one couple is a wonderful thing. Jesus thinks so too. "For this reason a man will leave his father and mother and be united to his wife," he said, "and the two will become one flesh. So they are no longer two, but one. Therefore what God has joined together, let man not separate."[1] That's mystifying!

The climate in our culture is tough on marriage, but don't give up the hope of a good marriage. If you go after it, you just might get in on the mystery of being one with another person.

A couple of hints:

• There are no operational manuals for marriage. What you learn at home may or may not prepare you for your own marriage. Know going in that you'll produce an original because you and your mate are originals.

• Expect it to take years, maybe a decade or more, of concentrated work to produce the kind of marriage that will still be happy after fifty or sixty years. Know that it's time well spent.

• The single most important element in a good marriage is friendship. Romance is up and down, physical attractiveness is subject to the law of gravity, success comes and goes, but friendship—ah, *friendship*. It grows and flowers to the end.

• Marriage is like a triangle with you and your mate at the bottom angles and God at the top. The closer each of you get to God, the closer you get to each other.

• Marriage isn't everything. It's very plausible that you might never marry and still live a magnificent life. Singleness is and has always been a reasonable option. So relax, get to know God, and see what happens.

See: Commitment, Living Together, Sex.

[1]Matthew 19:5-6.

MATERIALISM

To feel good, some people eat, get high, have sex, make money, or buy things. If finding pleasure in these ways becomes the focus of your life (i.e., you spend most of your money, time, or effort pursuing them), then you're materialistic.

The problem with materialism is that the pleasure it delivers is never quite enough to fill the need you have. What happens is you keep buying, eating, sleeping around, or whatever—but you never feel satisfied.

One of the most popular forms of materialism is *consumerism*, whose participants play by the rule, "Whoever dies with the most stuff wins." To play, you keep buying toys and clothes and stereos and records and shoes and electronic gadgets and computers and cars and anything else you think will give you pleasure, until you run out of money.

Unfortunately, companies that sell these things tell you in their advertising that their products will bring you the very things you feel you're missing on the inside: jeans that make every guy stop and pay attention, a car that identifies you as the classy person you think you are, shoes that let you fit in with the right crowd, a stereo that's the envy of your friends, toys that announce to the world that you know how to have fun. But if you've played this game at all, you know the bad news: the promises of the advertisers are nine-tenths empty.

But what's the good news?

If the material world cannot fill the need we have in our hearts, then there are two possibilities: either life is a cruel joke, a frustrating and pointless search for a satisfaction we can never have, or it's a time to discover that there's a spiritual side to us which, having been created by God, will never be satisfied until we are reunited with him.

According to Jesus (and he ought to know), the answer is this: "Everyone who drinks this water will be thirsty again, but whoever drinks the water I give him will never thirst. Indeed, the water I give him will become in him a spring of life welling up to everlasting life."[1] While Madonna sings, "We're living in a material world, and I am a material girl," the Police declare the truth: "We are spirits in the material world . . . there must be another way."

If you struggle with materialism, then find the needs in your heart that aren't being met and work with God so he can begin to fill them. He's waiting for your permission.

See: Money.

[1]John 4:13-14.

RAY'S THE NAME... RAY BAN

R.B.

MENOPAUSE

Imagine going through puberty backwards and you've got a hint at the physiological and emotional confusion that's produced by menopause. Sooner or later (usually in her late forties) a woman stops menstruating for good. It's a mixed blessing—the body and emotions do strange things for a while, but it's also the end of her monthly period.

A complicating factor is that women frequently begin menopause while they've got a pubescent kid in the house, which is fun only for those who enjoy clashing hormones.

When the lady of your home becomes menopausal, be generous. It's no fun for her, either.

MERCY

When you give someone what he deserves, that's justice. When you give a guilty person what he *doesn't* deserve, that's mercy.

Jesus was crucified along with two criminals whose crosses stood on either side of him. One of the criminals started shouting insults: "Aren't you the Christ? Save yourself and us!"

But the other criminal stopped him: "We are punished justly, for we are getting what our deeds deserve. [That's justice.] But this man has done nothing wrong." Then he turned to Jesus: "Remember me when you come into your kingdom."

Jesus answered him: "I tell you the truth, today you will be with me in paradise."[1] That's mercy. God's love is merciful—you don't deserve it. And what you *do* deserve, you don't have to accept—Christ accepted it for you, just like he accepted it for the criminal who asked him.

If you want to imitate Christ (that is, act as a Christian), love mercy. When a friend drops her lunch tray in the middle of the room (that's what she *gets* for being a klutz), clean it up for her. If someone lies to you, cheats you, or insults you, show him mercy. If someone could use your forgiveness, forgive him— forgiveness is a kind of mercy.

And what does the Lord require of you? "To act justly and to love mercy and to walk humbly with your God."[2]

More: Matthew 5:7; 18:21-35; James 2:13.

See: Justice.

[1]Luke 23:39-43.
[2]Micah 6:8.

MIDLIFE CRISIS

See: Parents.

MONDAY MORNING

It's the gateway to a solid week of work or school or both. It's the first of five days of early mornings and long days. It's the first moment during the course of the week that you have serious doubts about making it to Saturday—and all you did was wake up.

Monday morning is a time of faith. Although you

can't possibly figure out how you're going to survive the week, you look back to all of the other weeks you somehow outlived and decide to give it a try. You have to trust that the God who brought you this far is going to see you through this time, too. (It helps to know that God is beyond time and therefore never has Monday mornings. He's awake and ready to look after you every hour of every day.)

If Mondays are really tough for you, try these tricks:

• Take twenty minutes on Sunday night to go over your week in a calendar. Schedule what you've got to do and block out time for fun things, too. Lots of Monday-morning dread comes from imagining a busier week than you actually have to live. Your calendar will show you the truth.

• Schedule a fun activity for Mondays—a special lunch treat, an after-school adventure, a family dessert night where members alternate the responsibility of making dessert for the rest of the family.

• Make Mondays your servant day—imagine that everyone feels as bad as you, then do whatever you can to help them forget that it's Monday. Give back rubs, smile, laugh, hand out compliments, show concern, and hide encouraging notes for people to find later that day.

More: Psalm 61:1-3.

MONEY

Money is powerful stuff. How much you have has absolutely no effect on how happy you are, but what you *do* with your money has a lot to do with your happiness.

How to spend it:

Most of us don't seem to have any problem spending money; our problem is learning *not* to spend it! Here are ten tips that can help you spend money more wisely:

1. Ask yourself, "Why do I want this thing?" The real need may be greater than the product's ability to deliver. (See Materialism.)

2. Postpone buying decisions for one week for items over $5.

3. Never believe anyone who says that the deal is too good to pass up or that you'll never find as good a deal as the one you are being offered. Ninety-nine percent of the time it's not true, and you'll save more money passing up all these offers than you would save in that one-in-a-hundred unbeatable deal.

4. Arrange for your employer to direct-deposit your paycheck into your savings account.

5. Establish a savings account that requires two signatures for a withdrawal—yours and a family member.

6. Get your parents to deposit all your earnings, giving you a certain amount each week to live on. (This is a lot of work on their part—try doing it on your own first.)

7. Invite three good friends with responsible spending habits to be your financial advisers. Whenever you want to spend more than $25 on something, you must present the idea to them and receive their unanimous approval. If they object, you can't buy it.

8. Each morning put in your wallet only the

amount of money you know you'll need for that day's essentials. Keep the extra cash at home.

9. Hang around people who spend less. If the main social activity of your group of friends is shopping, chances are you're going to spend more money than you should.

10. Every time you spend even a penny, write down how much you spent and what you spent it on. This cuts down on your spending, because buying something isn't easy when you have to spend two minutes digging through your purse or pack for your expense book, and writing down your purchases makes you realize just how silly some of them really are. Hold a contest with yourself to see how little money you can live on each week. Each week that your total is less than the week before, treat yourself to a small reward that doesn't count against the next week's total.

How to invest it:

The easiest investment you can make is a savings account. Banks and savings and loans will pay better interest on your money if you deposit lots of it. If you don't have lots, consider pooling your money with other friends to create one account that qualifies for a higher interest rate. To avoid a mathematical nightmare, have everyone contribute the same amount and agree to withdraw the money after a set time. Either have one extremely trustworthy person act as trustee to the account, or open the account so that any withdrawal requires everyone's signature.

Be extremely cautious of "sure-fire" investment schemes. The better it sounds, the more skeptical you should be (and the more money this lesson is going to cost you if you're not). Remember this: if it sounds too good to be true, it probably is.

One of the best ways to invest money is to spend it on things that will help you make more money. Buy a snow blower, tool set, car-detailing equipment, baking equipment, or word processor—then clear driveways, fix stereos, detail cars, bake pies, or type papers for others. If the initial investment is too steep, team up with a friend and start a partnership. Work together or alternate the days that each is entitled to use the equipment.

How to give it:
That's right—*give* it. Giving money away is not so hard if you believe that everything you have really belongs to God anyway. Giving is a way of saying thanks for the opportunity to use God's money to meet your own needs and desires. Many people take a tenth of what they have and use it to give thanks for the nine-tenths they have the privilege of using. Other people give more than that—some giving nearly everything they have. (This percentage-giving is also called *tithing*, from an Old English word meaning *tenth*.)

The joy of giving is a thrilling act of faith. I've never been inside a prison, but I know I'm making a difference in the lives of prisoners because I give money to an organization that shares Christ's love inside prison walls. I've never been to Chile, but there's a little girl there who is eating well and getting a good education because of the money I send to sponsor her. The money I give each month to my church and other organizations is making a difference. I may be one of five billion people on this planet, but I feel significant because God is able to do so much with the portion of my income I give back to him.

If you're serious about giving, here are some hints to help you start:
• Keep a record of all your income.
• Decide on a day each week or month that you will give.
• Consider who you want to give to. Pray about needs you hear of through your church, youth group, family, friends, and school.
• Try to give to something on a regular basis over time. Your small amount (no matter how small) will make more of a difference because you'll be more likely to pray for that need each time you give.
• Don't be afraid to team up with friends to make your giving have a bigger impact. Four high-school students who couldn't individually afford to sponsor needy children in other countries joined forces—each of them chips in $5.25 every month to sponsor one child. That child now has not one, but *four* people in North America praying for his well-being!

How to borrow it:
If you borrow from somebody, give him an IOU showing how much you borrowed, when you borrowed it, and when he can expect to be paid back. This shows him that you appreciate the gesture, that you intend to pay it back, and that you give him the right to hold you to your end of the deal. Write out a copy for yourself and put the pay-back date on your calendar. If you mess up and can't pay back on the date you promised, tell the person *that day*—don't put him in the uncomfortable position of having to ask you for his own money. And don't put yourself in the

position of avoiding him. "Let no debt remain out-standing, except the continuing debt to love one another."[1]

If you are borrowing lots of money, entering into some kind of installment plan (e.g., making monthly payments on a stereo or car), or signing up for a credit card (only slightly cheaper than borrowing from a loan shark), make sure that you have a copy of the note. This note is just a fancy IOU describing the terms of the loan — principal (the amount of money you're borrowing), interest and fees (the cost of using someone else's money), when payments are due, penalties (if your payment is late), and any other tricks and details.

It's a good idea to have someone who understands financial agreements look over the paperwork for you before you sign it. Ask a parent, your math teacher, or the loan officer at your bank (they're the ones in the business suits who sit behind those big desks). If the person giving the loan (or selling the merchandise) won't let you take a copy to be looked over by one of these people until *after* you sign, get out while you still own a pen to sign with. They may tell you, "I can't hold this deal — it's now or never" or some such thing to make you feel it's urgent. Just yawn, relax, and walk away — no deal is so good it's worth getting snookered on.

How to lend it:

If you lend someone money, be ready for the possibility that you may never see it again. If you never get it back, then it's no surprise to you and a gift to the one who borrowed it. If you're repaid, then it's like getting a gift of money you never expected. It seems

like a strange way to handle money, but there are some good reasons for it.

First, if you're a Christian, it's not your money anyway—it's God's money, and he's letting someone else use it. Second, if the borrower is a friend, then God prefers that you keep the friendship and lose the money rather than keep the money and lose the friendship; if you expect it back, you're liable to lose both. Third, if the borrower is an enemy, then you have the opportunity to demonstrate the kind of selfless love that is God's specialty; God is most pleased when we act most like him. (We're not making this stuff up—you can read it for yourself in Matthew 5:42 and Luke 6:34-36.)

If you see a double standard here (you're expected to repay your loans, but you can't expect others to pay back theirs), then you have discovered one of the basic principles of the faith: Christ calls you to be a servant. That is, you *choose* to treat others better than yourself. "If anyone wants to be first, he must be the very last, and the servant of all."[2] (What kind of a servant would you be if you expected the same treatment as those you served?) Count it a privilege that you don't have to worry about others getting a better deal than you. Everything you give to others is repaid to you in heaven, and anything you could possibly receive on this earth by being treated equally is worthless in comparison to that.

[1]Romans 13:8.
[2]Mark 9:35.

MOTHER

See: Parents.

THE MYTH OF INVINCIBILITY

"It can't happen to me." That's the Myth of Invincibility. You've seen it a thousand times—kids jumping trains, driving too fast, driving under the influence, playing with fire (literally and figuratively). There's evidence that a lot of pregnancies result from the myth that says, "Oh, I'm too young or too careful to have a baby." Yeah, right. The myth is why your auto insurance is so high, and it's the source of a good many broken bones and not a few broken hearts.

This is not to say you should spend your life in bed because the world is too dangerous to get up and out. If your life doesn't pass before your eyes every now and again, you may forget you're alive.

Take some risks. But take smart risks. Learn the limits of your mortality, and don't push the limits that can cost you your life. Just about every town in America has a tree draped with sad ribbons and dead flowers—a memorial to some kid who drove too fast and pushed too hard. A monument to the Myth of Invincibility.

More: Psalm 90.

NERDS

See: Normal?, Prejudice.

NO

See: Saying No.

NORMAL?

You have an image of what's normal, and the more you think about it, the more you're convinced you don't fit it. You're not like everyone else, and what scares you even more is that you don't *want* to be like them.

The World Series was last week—*everybody* watches the World Series. You didn't watch it. You didn't even know who was playing. All your friends wear a certain style of shoe—you think they look silly. Neither can you find what's so fascinating in the kind of music they listen to. When it comes to movies, your tastes are so opposite that you don't even bother to go to a movie unless they say it was horrible. You were the only one in the history of your school who enjoyed studying Israel's Six-Day War. And you ride a unicycle.

Are you normal? Yes. Your tastes are different than those of your peers, but there's nothing wrong with that. You're human, and God gave you your own tastes and perceptions. Thank him for your uniqueness. Each person has unique tastes, and as you get to know your friends better, you'll see them as different (but normal), too.

NUCLEAR WAR

The most disgusting part of war is that it often kills the innocent—citizens whose only crime was to be in the wrong place at the wrong time. The Bible is very clear in pointing out that the shedding of innocent blood is wrong. (See Genesis 9:6; Matthew 27:4, 24-25.) If war is ever justified (it's *never* good, but many believe it is sometimes a necessary evil), then we must do everything we can to prevent the shedding of innocent blood. But in a nuclear war, how can we do that? Nuclear bombs are indiscriminate—they kill military personnel and private citizens and any other living thing within miles of ground zero. A country with a nuclear bomb is like a gunman taking hostages: shoot at him and he'll kill some innocent people.

Unfortunately, the previous generation has left you with tens of thousands of these bombs—and you must decide what to do with them. For some Christian principles that you can use to shape your decision, see Justice, Mercy, Taking a Stand.

PARENTS

No matter what we say about parents, we're in for big trouble. If we say negative things, we'll get loud protests from kids who reserve the right to criticize their parents themselves, but won't allow anybody else to make a crack about Mum and get away with it. And if we say positive things, we'll hear from the disgruntled who think we'd take a different view if we had to live with *their* old man.

Still, we need to say *something*, so here are a few thoughts that might help you as well as your parents:

First, remember that your mom and dad are human. It doesn't get any more complicated (or more simple) than that. They're made of the same stuff you are, with the same hopes, the same apprehensions, and same failures. In fact, if you want to know what you'll be like as a parent (while you're still in a position to do something about it), ask your parents to describe themselves when they were teenagers. Chances are they were a lot *then* like they are *now*—

only younger. Think about it. Someday you, too, will be an older, more intense version of what you are now.

If you're uncomfortable with the idea of being more like yourself as you grow older, *now* is the time to do something about it. You can change.

Second, the only way for you to achieve independence from your parents is to achieve a kind of interdependence *with* your parents—develop a good relationship with them, in other words. What your parents are trying to do (whether they realize it or not) is to work themselves out of a job and raise an adult. They will know they've succeeded when they feel they can relate to you as a friend, a peer. It takes time—it doesn't happen overnight. But it will happen if you want it to.

Wouldn't it be nice to sit down someday with your parents for a cup of coffee and some good conversation rather than to explain one more time why you didn't take out the trash or clean your room?

A third thought about parents: for a lot of fathers, midlife hits like a ton of bricks, and rarely do they see it coming. Everything seems fine until your dad starts wondering if he'll ever really make it in his profession. Or maybe he made it, and he wonders why he worked so hard to achieve . . . *this*?

He may look in the mirror and (shock!) gravity has taken control. He starts to look like a toddler again—his chest is again smaller than his belly. His thighs are flabby. (Weren't they firm and powerful once? He can't remember.)

As they watch their children entering their prime, some men try to recapture theirs with a sports car, a fitness club, skydiving, more work, or a younger woman.

If your dad is handling his midlife gracefully and with good humor, be thankful and supportive. If he isn't handling it so well, he needs to know more than ever that you love him in spite of it all. (See Menopause.)

Fourth: Allow your parents to grow. Kids are often less tolerant of change than parents are, which is understandable: kids need stability in order to feel safe. But your parents may need a career change, a new hairdo, or a new hobby in order to feel alive and healthy again. A change in your parents may be frightening to you, but remember—if they're happier, you'll be happier. Give them a lot of encouragement.

Finally, make time to be with your parents. They need to touch base with you, to know you're okay so they'll know they're okay. Make a habit of spending a little time with them every week. It may be tough, but it's worth it. If they seem too busy for you, get creative. Call your mom's secretary and get an appointment under an assumed name (then go out for some ice cream). Kidnap your dad on a Saturday morning and take him someplace weird for breakfast. You're smart—you'll find a way.

More: Ephesians 6:1-3; Hebrews 12:4-12.

See: Accountability, Divorce, Stepparents.

PARTY

Balloons, streamers, birthday cake, punch, clowns, and pony rides. Parties like that were good, clean fun because . . . well, because they were good, clean fun. The worst thing you could do was spill punch on your new dress or wet your pants on the pony. But by the time many high schoolers start planning their own parties, they forget the "good" and the "clean" and just concentrate on the "fun" — and some even forget this. Some people even use the word *party* in a way that seems synonymous with sleazy. Maybe it's time we changed the meaning back to what it used to be — celebration.

You have three choices when it comes to parties.

• Don't go. This is a wise choice if what's going on there will cause you (or the person you bring) to get into trouble.

• Go and be a positive influence. If you can serve God this way without compromising your values, then this may be worth considering.

• Plan good, clean-fun parties of your own. Give your friends an alternative to going out and getting drunk. Create fun parties that celebrate life, build up relationships, and give friends a healthy escape from the pressures of the week.

See: Friday Night.

PEER PRESSURE

See: Imaginary Audience.

PMS

Premenstrual Syndrome is no joke. Most girls tolerate some changes around the time of menstruation every month, but girls who suffer from PMS endure radical changes that make life miserable for days at a time.

Imagine feeling so anxious that you're not sure you can cope with simple tasks, bursting into tears for no identifiable cause, or screaming at someone you love for no good reason. Frustration.

Imagine gaining five pounds in a couple of days, craving food, breaking out, losing all motivation. Confusion.

PMS produces these and other strange symptoms in otherwise stable, reliable people — and if they seem overwhelmed by it all, no wonder.

If you suffer from PMS, talk with your doctor about it. She may have some good advice, maybe even a booklet you can read. Mark your calendar for a few months and note any patterns that emerge in your physical and emotional well-being. Reassure yourself that you're not going crazy by referring to the calendar and doing sanity checks with people who know you well, especially in your household. Watch the kind of food you eat around your period: beware of sugar, salt, and caffeine. Remember who you really are, nurture a sense of humor, tell God about your frustration.

If you live with a PMS sufferer, be generous. She needs you.

More: Niels H. Lauersen, *PMS: Premenstrual Syndrome and You* (Simon & Schuster, 1983).

POSSESSIVENESS

Possessiveness begins with attaching the word *my* to the front of a relationship: "My friend, my youth group, my girlfriend." It's hard to tell when you've crossed the line between healthy pride in a relationship that says, "Oh yeah, we're going out. He's really something isn't he!" and the sort of ownership that says, "Yeah, he's mine—stay away from him!"

No relationship can survive possessiveness for very long. It's too much pressure. People can't breathe if they're held too tightly.

But there's a bigger issue. Most people depend on the things they own (and the people they "own") for their identity and security. But just as great wardrobes and new cars ultimately fail to make people secure, so, too, do other people.

Possessiveness may be evidence of a deep empty place in your life—the fear, perhaps, that you will be alone if you don't try to fill the empty place yourself. On a strictly human level, you know you can't really possess another person—not if you love her. If you love someone, the saying goes, set them free.

And on a deeper level, consider this thought from Blaise Pascal, the seventeenth-century physicist who did the original research on vacuums: "In the heart of every man there is a God-shaped vacuum that can only be filled by God in the person of his Son, Jesus Christ." We're called upon to open the empty places, and *he* will fill them. And we're called upon to imitate him in our relationships, treating our friends as he has treated us. If you love someone . . .

See: Breaking Up, Dating.

POVERTY

See: Compassion.

PRAYER

Prayer is communicating with God: talking, listening, laughing, crying, asking questions, saying thanks. Praying is a long walk with very few words; it may also be a yelp of terror, too quick for words. A couple of encouraging ideas about praying:

• You're *talking* with God. This is no Now-I-lay-me-down-to-sleep kind of exercise. It's interaction with God! The time and place and words are of no importance compared with the act of communicating with him.

• God is listening. If you think you've got to get God's attention, relax. You have it. It is his pleasure to hear you and to answer because that's the sort of person he is. Jesus said, "If you then, though you are evil, know how to give good gifts to your children, how much more will your Father in heaven give the Holy Spirit to those who ask Him!"[1] Don't misunderstand. God is not sitting up in heaven like a cosmic Coke machine. He is more interested in what you need than in what you want, and he knows the difference better than you. But know this: he *is* listening. You have his full attention.

• Jesus prayed. In Jesus we see a person in intimate contact with his heavenly Father. Note as you read the New Testament that Jesus doesn't *do* miracles — he *prays*, and his Father does them. Jesus prayed to interact with his Father. And that is simply the way we can interact with our Father. "This is how you should pray:" Jesus said, " 'Our Father in heaven . . . ' "[2] When do you communicate with someone? Whenever you're together. When are you ever *not* together with your heavenly Father?

More: John 14:1-14; Philippians 4:4-7; 1 John 5:13-15.

See: Abba.

[1]Luke 11:13.
[2]Matthew 6:9.

PREGNANCY

Pregnancy is one portion of a miracle that stretches itself over three-fourths of a year, from conception to childbirth. The miracle is the creation of life.

PREJUDICE

Prejudice starts out as a judgment made without the facts. That's a horrible way of judging. How would you feel if your English teacher graded a stack of papers by assigning an A to the top one, a B to the next, a C to the next, then a D, then an F, then another A, and so on through the stack? The grades would have no relationship to the quality of the papers. But we make equally ridiculous judgments. People often hold a prejudice against a racial group when they have never met even *one person* of that race.

A judgment made without the facts, if allowed to go unquestioned, won't be affected when the facts are finally known. You know that the sun doesn't literally rise and set. It doesn't do anything but sit there while you ride around on one side of a spinning earth and get glimpses of it during part of the ride. But does this fact get in the way of your judgment? Have you ever been to an Easter Earthturn service?

Whether you call a particular phenomenon a sunrise or an earthturn isn't going to harm too many people. But when you *know* that gender has no effect on one's intelligence, yet choose to act as if does, you've let a prejudice stand in the way of your Christian behavior. A prejudice, having progressed from a mere lack of facts to a total disregard of them, is extremely hard to overcome.

Don't let prejudice get its hook in you before you find the facts. Look for injustice, and you'll probably find a prejudice just under the surface.

See: Justice.

PRIORITIES

When the chips are down, your back is against the wall, and you have to make a hard choice, you go with your priorities. It's as simple as that.

A wise teacher observed, "What you do stands behind you, thundering all the while, so that I cannot hear what you say." Talk is cheap.

People don't have to ask you what's important in your life. They have eyes. By watching how you spend your time and money, they can soon make an educated guess about your real values.

Write your five top priorities on a sheet of paper. Be as honest and complete as you can about the commitments you hold.

Now let's play "Man From Mars." Imagine that an alien has been watching you for the last six weeks. What would *he* say are your priorities? Why?

If the man from Mars sees you as you see yourself, congratulations! You know yourself pretty well. If not, you've got your work cut out for you.

One other wrinkle. How do you think your priorities match God's priorities? Your answer to this question may be the very heart of the matter.

More: Matthew 6:25-34; Psalm 50.

PRIVATE PARTS

Remember the first year you dressed out for gym?

Some boys saunter naked through rows of lockers toward the showers, towel flung carelessly over one shoulder, confident, puberty on parade.

Others make their way like thieves in an alley, towel clutched carefully, strategically hanging from the navel.

Waiting for the next available showerhead one boy examines his lip and jaw in a mirror. "Probably start shaving soon," he mumbles to no one in particular. Nearby a boy concentrates on soaping up without raising his elbows so no one will notice the absence of hair under his arms.

On the other side of the building, meanwhile, a girl all but climbs into her locker to change into her gym clothes. She listens to a couple of people making brassiere jokes and fails to see the humor. Her biggest worry is related to the story she heard about a girl who got her first menstrual period at school and wasn't prepared. "What if that happens to me?"

Almost everybody worries about their private parts. Boys, wondering if it's normal to wake up in a pool of semen, quietly change their sheets in the middle of the night. (It is normal—it's called a *nocturnal emission* and is evidence that puberty has begun. That nocturnal emissions are sometimes associated with erotic dreams demonstrates the intimate connection of mind and body.) When lumps appear behind their nipples, girls wonder, "Is this cancer?" (No, it's the beginning of breast enlargement.) When one breast seems to grow sooner or faster than the other, they worry, "Is this normal?" (Yep, it sure is.)

If you've been nervous about whether or not you are developing normally, take heart. People mature at different rates, all of which are "normal." Don't compare your development to the person in your class who is voted most likely to be mistaken for a Marine (or most likely to date a Marine). Look at the whole range of people, and—if you fit in more or less with other people your age—relax.

And if you don't fit within the developmental range of the other people your age, talk with someone you trust. If you're not comfortable asking your mom or dad, how about your doctor? Or maybe there's a teacher you trust or the youth worker at your church. If there's nothing wrong, they can help you find that out. And if there is something wrong, they'll help you get the treatment you need to make it right.

More: Psalm 139:11-16.

See: Adolescence, Normal?

PROM

Know the source of the word prom? It's an abbreviation of the word *promenade*: "A walk, especially in a public place as for pleasure or display."[1]

Sociologist Tony Campolo wonders if prom night isn't the night of the year when *everybody* knows who's got it and who doesn't. The people with dates are in and the people without dates are out. Can that be right?

Ever wonder why so many relationships get underway just in time for the prom? And so many hold on just long enough to get through the prom?

And so many couples break up a couple of weeks before the prom? And so few relationships endure very long past the prom?

How much money do you suppose will be spent at your school for the prom this year?

A true story: Ten high schoolers decided to go to the prom together. Each had a responsibility for the night—flowers, dinner, breakfast, transportation, entertainment. They ate a fancy meal at the home of a youth worker, had a squirt-gun fight in the park, and cooked breakfast on a camping stove about dawn. The prom itself was the low-light of a magnificent night—but it gave them an excuse to dress up.

The prom is what you make it.

[1]*New Century Dictionary* (Appleton-Century-Crofts, 1957).

PUBERTY

See: Adolescence, PMS, Private Parts.

RACISM

See: Prejudice.

RAPE

Let's get right to the point on this: rape is not sex, it's violence. About thirty percent of adult women in America have been forced into a sexual encounter against their will. That's one in three. And the numbers aren't shrinking at present, which means—well, think about the three girls you know best and imagine one of them being forced into a sexual act.

The popular image is of a stranger coming out of the dark to force himself on a woman. That happens, of course. But *much* more commonly, the rapist is someone the girl knows and trusts. A couple of other popular ideas:

• "She was asking for it." No she wasn't. Nobody asks to be brutalized.

• "She wasn't raped, he was just messing around with her. He didn't go all the way." Sexual assault is so near rape it's hard to tell the difference.

Rape makes a person feel *alone*. And many rape victims carry the emotional burden of the violence alone. Sometimes it's because she doesn't know how to talk about it or who to tell. Frequently, the victim remains alone because she's been hurt by someone she knows—a date, an acquaintance, even a relative—and she doesn't know what to do with that.

Being raped doesn't increase a person's ability to trust.

If you've been raped: Don't carry it alone—even if it was a year ago or more. Find someone you trust and tell her. If the person you tell knows you well, it won't come as a massive surprise. She noticed when you withdrew; she could tell something was wrong; she may even have reached out to you. When you confide in that person, you'll be giving the missing piece to a puzzle she is already eager to solve. You probably want to try to forget, hoping it will take care of itself.

It won't. Your trust has been broken, you've been brutalized. Nobody should go through that alone.

If you know someone who has been raped: What your friend needs is support of the most understanding and substantial kind. That means listening more than talking. You don't have to know the right thing to say—just be the right person to talk to. (See When You Don't Know What To Say.) Find out how she feels. If she says it's no big deal, that's probably because she wishes it were no big deal. Perhaps you can go with her to talk with an adult you both trust or even find the support of other young women who have suffered rape. (Ask around; you'll find some-one who knows where to look.)

More: Judges 19 and 20. (Careful—it's not pretty.)

RUMORS

See: Gossip.

RUNNING AWAY

Most teenagers run away when their home situations become absolutely unbearable. When they run, they leave with the clothes on their backs, rushing away from crises that seem to have no solutions. Whatever it was that pushed them over the edge, they felt that anything was better than staying home. The sad truth is most of them run *to* situations infinitely worse than the ones they ran *from*.

If your home situation is bad, do something about it now. Don't wait until you're so desperate that you run. If you're being abused—sexually, physically, psychologically—then get help. Talk to a trusted adult. You don't have to go through this, and you don't deserve abuse.

If you want to get your parents' attention, try other ways. If they won't listen to you, get a counselor or a minister to set up a meeting with all of you so you can get some things discussed.

If you feel you have no other choice but to run, run to the family of a friend—don't spend a night on the street. The stories kids tell of their experiences on the street are scarier than any horror film—most of us can't begin to imagine what it's like to live through such nightmares. You never want to find out.

See: Help.

SAFE SEX

Is there any? Can putting a condom between two people ensure the safety of their encounter? Probably not.

We're asked to assume that sexual contact is merely physical, that sex is disconnected from emotional and spiritual considerations. Does anyone believe that anymore? Oh, there are people who *act* like they believe it, but almost everybody knows we're not rutting pigs, all excited because we've come into heat and it's taken us by breathless surprise.

Sex is more than sexual contact. Sex is intimacy and implied permanence. Sex is an expression of personal commitment—and *that's* not safe. So sex with a virtual stranger, even with a condom, is certainly not safe).

You risk more than AIDS or pregnancy when you make the kind of commitment that's required by sexual intimacy: you risk yourself—how you see yourself and how someone else will see you from now on.

Imagine the confusion in a person who is sixteen years old and has taken that risk with three or four people. She's got the uneasy, unhappy feeling that she's lost something she'll never get back, and, of course, she's right.

More: 1 Corinthians 6:9-20.

See: Abortion, Sex, Technical Virginity.

SAYING NO

When you say yes to some things, you automatically say no to some others. You don't even really have to think about it. "Yes" to friendship is "No" to gossip and unfaithfulness. "Yes" to Jesus is "No" to anything or anybody that would challenge or replace him. Sometimes you can tell how convincingly a person has said yes to a relationship or commitment by how easy it is for her to say no to the people and things that threaten to undo that commitment (whether it's the tennis team, a romance, or her interaction with Christ).

Some of us like to please other people so much that we feel uncomfortable saying no when we're asked to do something. And some of us are experience junkies who are suckers for an opportunity. The thought of missing the next big one drives us to say yes even when we know we shouldn't.

Sometimes it's relatively harmless, like when you blow off studying to talk on the telephone. Sometimes it's costly, like when you fail a class because you blew off homework too often. Saying yes when you should've said no is disastrous when you do something dangerous or mean or compromising.

Sometimes we have to say no to good things. Good can be the enemy of best. When everyone around you says yes, you may still have to say no—and that's hard.

Make your decisions in advance. When a friend shoves a can of beer in your hand and asks you to drink up, when you find out your boyfriend's parents aren't home after all, when someone shoves a joint in your hand at a concert, you may not have a lot of time to think. So think in advance. If you don't know what to think, get help: read, ask questions, pray.

In a pinch, the surest way to say no is to leave. Think about that. Strike a bargain with your parents or a trusted friend so that you've got a way out of tough spots. If you're in trouble tonight, get relief *tonight*. You can put things back together tomorrow.

More: Romans 6, especially verses 11-13; Hebrews 10:19-25.

See: Accountability, Commitment, 502, Help, Substance Abuse.

School

"Don't let school get in the way of your education."—Joseph Bayly, the late Christian publishing executive, novelist, and journalist.

See: GPA, Study.

SELF-IMAGE

See: Abba, Imaginary Audience, Normal?, Steroids.

SELFISHNESS

Selfishness is not a bad habit that you learn—you were an expert at it from the moment you were born. One of life's toughest challenges is trying to lose your expertise.

When you're completely selfish, life revolves around *you*; other people have meaning only when they affect your happiness. Or the way a friend of ours puts it, "But enough about me; what do *you* think about me?"

In a way, selfishness is a form of idolatry. The deity you worship is the one in the mirror: to that idol you sacrifice most of your money, time, dreams, and desires. It's a painless sacrifice, because you're really giving the riches of your life to yourself. It's also a worthless sacrifice, because no matter how much you give to your self-god, it will never be able to give you what you really want. Like a broken slot machine, all the riches you ever give it will never make it pay out a jackpot. (See Materialism.)

If the wrong god has been getting most of your attention lately, rearrange your schedule. Figure out what you have to give the *right* God (hint: look for what he has given you), and then give it to him each day. Do you have free time? Give him a chunk of it each week by volunteering somewhere—a church, a

hospital, a community center for handicapped children. Do you have money? Give a portion of it each
month to organizations that are changing people's
lives. Do you have friends and family? Give them
your prayers, laughter, and labors each day. Do you
have the gift of listening well? Empathy? The ability

to speak, write, create, or manage others? Give whatever you've got, and use it all to share the love of God with those around you.

More: Matthew 25:31-46; 2 Corinthians 5:15.

See: Servanthood.

SERIOUS

"Why did you guys break up?"

"Well, he's a nice guy and everything; it's just that things were getting too serious."

"Oh. I know what you mean."

Yeah, we all know what she means. It's amazing that most of the relationships that make it past the typical breakup hazards like selfishness and loss of interest, get caught on this one. It's as if there's a built-in barrier that'll get you now or get you later.

In a way that's true. It's rare for people in their teens to have the kind of relationship that can endure for a lifetime together (not non-existent, of course, but rare). And one of the big trials is the Serious test.

Put simply: you know it's getting too serious if you're starting to act married. That means that if you're progressing into married sexual territory, it's getting too serious. And if you can't make plans without consulting each other, it's getting too serious.

So how do you keep a relationship from getting too serious?

• If you're sixteen, act like it. Sixteen-year-olds are not generally marriageable in our culture; and in the ones where they are, the weddings are normally arranged by parents. Hold on to sixteen as long as you can.

• Tell the truth. Getting to know someone is not the same as loving him. Going to the prom is not a commitment, it's a date.

• Date in groups. There's safety in numbers.

• Dream your dreams out loud so there will be no misunderstanding. Where do you want to be in five years? What do you want to do with your life? Dreaming out loud should make you more interesting, and if it's a threat then maybe things are already too serious.

See: Breaking Up.

SERVANTHOOD

God has a delightful way of turning the world's systems topsy-turvy: the Savior of the world was born in a stable, his country-bumpkin disciples out-taught the best professors around, and one of his worst enemies became the most prolific author in the New Testament. One of the greatest flip-flops was what he did to the rules of leadership—"If anyone wants to be first, he must be the very last, and the servant of all."[1]

One time Jesus got down and washed the feet of all of his disciples to show them what he meant by this servanthood stuff (drastically new concepts call for drastic lessons). Aren't you glad he went through such pain to show us what true leadership is all about? What a shame it would be if this message of leading by serving never made it to the twentieth century.

The way servanthood works is simple: anyone you're supposed to lead is someone you serve. If you supervise someone at your job, you're his servant. That means *your* job is to make sure he gets everything he needs to be happy and successful at *his* job. If he needs encouragement, instruction, laughter, or a listening ear, you serve it to him. And like any good servant, you anticipate needs rather than wait around for the servant's bell to ring. In fact, corporations that subscribe to this form of leadership (some think it's a new idea!) draw an upside-down organizational chart: the president and board of directors are on the *bottom* of the chart, the rest of the workers appear at various levels above them, and the customers sit at the top. Each person is hired to serve the people directly above them on the chart.

More: Matthew 20:20-28; John 13:12-15; Philippians 2:3-11.

[1]Mark 9:35.

Sex

C.S. Lewis put sex in perspective: "Suppose you came to a country where you could fill a theatre by simply bringing a covered plate on to the stage and then slowly lifting the cover so as to let every one see, just before the lights went out, that it contained a mutton chop or a bit of bacon, would you not think that in that country something had gone wrong with the appetite for food?"[1] Indeed.

Don't make the mistake of believing that sex is everything or that sex is nothing.

We know it's not everything because plenty of people live satisfying lives without a sexual encounter for years at a time (hard as that is to believe). There is certainly a period of time in which the sexual appetite seems to be in perpetual motion. But when boiling hormones slow to a simmer, sexual desire takes its place in line with a whole range of appetites.

But sex is not nothing, either. It's an intimate expression of commitment—so intimate that the Bible assumes that the context for sex is the no-holds-barred honesty and all-out commitment of marriage. Outside that context sex takes on threatening proportions.

Unfair? Well, anybody can get behind the wheel of a car, but most of us want drivers to be licensed before we share the streets with them. If you need evidence of the dangerous potential of unmarried sex, consider herpes simplex, AIDS, an unwanted pregnancy, a broken heart.

Nobody understands the personal and interpersonal ramifications of being as intimate with someone as you are in sexual contact. If there's any human experience that calls for careful attention to the ways of God, this is it.

More: 1 Corinthians 6:12-20.

See: Homosexuality, Living Together, Marriage, Pregnancy, Rape, Safe Sex, Technical Virginity.

[1]C.S. Lewis, *Mere Christianity* (Macmillan, 1964).

SEXISM

See: Prejudice.

SHYNESS

A word of advice from a shy person:

I'm not shy

It's okay to be shy. If someone told you that it was wrong, he was probably an outgoing person, and the rest of us were too shy to argue with him. But I feel pretty bold as I sit alone in my office and write this, so I'm not afraid to tell you that shyness is a personality trait. Sure, some say that we shy folk need to come out of our shells a little more often, and that may be true. But I can think of a few outgoing people that would do well to climb back in their shells every so often.

As with any character trait, shyness has its disadvantages. If you're shy, you have to be careful not to appear conceited, because some people might read your quiet hesitation as a sign that you don't care for their company. Your smile is the best way to convey the truth: shy people smile—conceited people smirk, frown, or stare in mirrors. Another way to overcome a misperception is to be honest with your behavior. When I'm introduced to someone, I prefer to just be my awkward self rather than try to hide it. The other person immediately senses my shyness, and then does everything in his power to make me feel comfortable. I feel more at ease with him and forget my awkwardness. This method has become so much more comfortable for me that I'm beginning to act less awkward—which is a shame, since we shy ones are sought after for companionship because it is widely believed (and rightly so) that "still waters run deep," and I don't want to lose that.

SIN

Sin is when you choose to do something your way instead of God's way. It's a decision to be selfish. Here are a few other facts about sin that might interest you:
• If sin is selfishness, then you probably sin many times every day. If selfishness was only rudeness (like burping at the dinner table), then you would need only to be excused. But selfishness is sin—and sin requires forgiveness.
• You need to ask for God's forgiveness regularly. Telling him your sin makes *you* more aware of it, and that helps you to stop sinning.

• You need to pray constantly. This helps you remember who you're making each decision for, and it allows the Holy Spirit to guide you away from selfishness.

• You need to form good habits. If you had to consciously consider *every* decision you made, you'd never survive your first day. But if many of those decisions were made automatically by habit, you could concentrate on the special choices that have no quick answer.

• The more you obey God and try to do his will, the more like him you become. And the more like him you become, the more aware you become of your own sins—which is why spiritually mature people see themselves as sinful, while people with less mature faiths have a tough time identifying sin in their own lives.

See: Selfishness.

SPIRITUALITY

A paradox is a statement that seems contradictory but may be true at closer look. The Christian faith is full of paradoxes: the first will be last, you have to lose your life to find it, you become free from sin but slaves to God, you must die in order to live. The subject of spirituality seems to attract a herd of paradoxes. A friend of ours, Mike Yaconelli, has listed a few of the paradoxes he has observed:

• The more spiritual someone acts, the less spiritual he really is.

• Those who know all the answers to spiritual questions, really don't know.

- The closer you get to God, the farther you see there is still to go.
- The more spiritual questions you have, the closer you are to God.
- Once you've made it to the top, you realize you're not at the top.

Like physical growth, it's really difficult to feel yourself growing spiritually since it takes place slowly. And because God is so magnificent, you can't help but feel your own smallness through the whole process. In a world of instant results, spiritual growth seems like it takes forever—which is precisely how long it does take.

You don't doubt your own physical growth because you've seen photos of your childhood and touched miniature shoes that actually used to fit you. Keep spiritual memories by writing in a journal every so often. As you look back on these snapshots, you'll be able to see how much you've grown.

Spirituality, put simply, is becoming like Jesus. It's laughing at the things that make him laugh, and being heartbroken over the things that break his heart. To know these things, you've got to study him. That means reading his biography (the Gospels), studying from those he taught (they wrote the rest of the New Testament), and from those who predicted his coming (the Old Testament). You don't have to study alone—lots of people are serious about knowing and imitating Jesus, and studying with them can help you immensely. Listen to sermons. Attend a Bible study. Find someone who reminds you of Jesus (they're rare, but easy to identify) and watch him or her. The best way to do this is to find a spiritual mentor—a godly man or a godly woman—who can

act as a coach and adviser to teach you what he or she knows about Jesus. Try to meet with your mentor on a regular basis. If you need help finding a mentor, ask your church youth worker or minister for the name of someone who might be willing to help you.

Studying Jesus also means *talking* to him—which gives you a definite edge over those who have chosen to study anyone else who lived two thousand years ago. Ask him to help you see things through his eyes.

Nothing pleases him more than to see you trying to imitate him.

"And we, who with unveiled faces all reflect the Lord's glory, are being transformed into his likeness with ever-increasing glory, which comes from the Lord, who is the Spirit." (2 Corinthians 3:18.)

STEPPARENTS

Living with a stepparent seems a lot like a cold war to most people. "This person who is *not* my mom comes in and wants to *act* like my mom and that's just not going to happen. The first time she tells me what to do, I'm going to tell her . . . !"

It's a threat when a new person comes into your family. It's not just that he's not your real dad, it's also that he's sleeping with your real mom—doing all the things, in fact, that you're used to having your dad do. Many people find that very uncomfortable and usually deal with it badly. Some take a wait-and-see attitude that feels like you're going through International Customs just to say good morning. Others test the newcomer or get abusive in response to some very confused feelings. It's no picnic—but then it's no picnic for the stepparent, either.

Here are the hard facts: about sixty percent of second marriages end in divorce, and closer to seventy percent of third tries. The big strain on a second marriage can be children. That means, in addition to learning to live with a new spouse, that the couple must also be effective parents. That's a hard task made tougher by the fact that one of them isn't really your parent.

No matter how unwelcome they may be, step-parents are real people with real needs and hopes and dreams. It's unlikely that you've got a genuine wicked stepmother so, please, give her your courtesy and honesty, and acknowledge that you both want what's best for your family. It may be hard for you, but take the risk. Your stepparent could turn out to be a wonderful person.

More: Romans 12:9-21.

See: Divorce.

STEROIDS

It is very likely someone on your campus is selling steroids out of the trunk of his car. And students are buying them because steroids will bulk you up so fast it'll make a coach's head swim with dreams of a state championship. But steroids are scary business.

Like anything you buy from an uncertain source, you don't really know what you're getting. Buying steroids, even from a friend, is as dangerous as buying cocaine. You don't know what is really there.

Steroids make you grow like crazy by radically altering your body chemistry by introducing artificial-growth and sex hormones. Possible side effects:

- A decrease in normal male hormone levels that may decrease sperm count and sex drive.
- Premature stoppage of normal growth hormones so that users may end up shorter than they would have been.
- Premature, permanent balding.
- High blood pressure.
- Increased risk of liver disease.
- Heart attacks.

Steroids alter more than your hormones—they also alter the way you feel about yourself and others to the point that you may not be able to trust what's going on inside you in relationship with your friends, your family, your Savior.

Besides that, buying and selling steroids is illegal without the proper licensing. (Why do you think they're being sold out of the trunks of cars?). Steroids are dangerous. Anyone who tells you differently is full of bull.

STUDY

Everybody expects you to know how to study. It's like, "He's a junior in high school! He *knows* what to do. He's just lazy!"

The truth is, a lot of people get low grades not because they're stupid but because they lack some basic studying skills. Here are a few worth mastering.

In the classroom:

• If you have trouble concentrating in a class, ask for a new seating assignment. Ask to be placed front and center or as close to that as possible. That's worth half a grade by itself.

• Take notes of *some* kind. If you need to draw pictures of what the teacher is saying, do it. Write the nouns and verbs you hear. That may be enough to remind you of what or who is important.

• If your energy is consistently low in one class, eat some raisins or peanuts just before class begins.

Taking tests:

• Read the instructions and *especially* the questions thoroughly. Don't miss points because you answered what you *thought* was the question.

• Relax as much as you can. You know whatever you know. Coming apart during a test won't help you perform any better.

• If you're hung up on a problem or question, leave it. You can come back after you've finished what you're sure about. Don't throw away points you would've gotten had you not spent twenty minutes on a question you ended up guessing at anyway.

• On essay questions, choose an angle and get to the point. Write an outline lightly in the margin to remind you of where you're going.

• If there's time, look over your test before you turn it in. You may catch a simple mistake or get a sudden inspiration.

At home:
• Do it now! In most cases the only reason for cramming is that you've put off doing the work until the last minute. That's just not necessary. If you'll study first, before you watch TV, before you make phone calls, before you hang out, you'll get the work done faster and with greater quality.

• Study until you're finished—but when you *are* finished, quit, leave it alone, relax, play, feed your spirit. If you have to choose between pulling an all-nighter before a test and getting reasonable sleep, go with the sleep. You'll make the grade one way or the other.

• Determine the best environment for your study time and go with that as consistently as possible. If you're not distracted by your surroundings, you'll work faster. That almost certainly means that you need to study without the television or the radio (though there's evidence that some people do study better if they shut out the distracting sounds around them with music). Be sure to include adequate light.

Finally, develop an attitude that says, "I'm *going* to learn something from this class," especially if you hate the subject. Dare them to bore you! Your time is too valuable not to find a way to get something out of a class. If all else fails, try extra credit. Tell the teacher you're having trouble with the class and ask if there's another angle you can tackle outside to earn some extra credit. If nothing else, that might open some dialogue with your teacher.

More: Steve and Alice Lawhead, *The Ultimate Student Handbook* (Crossway Books, 1984).

SUBSTANCE ABUSE

Everybody's addicted to something. Some are addicted to drugs, some are addicted to alcohol, some say they are addicted to sex. Right.

One guy kicked the tobacco habit only to take up heavy eating. When the nicotine urge hits him at ten o'clock at night, he heads for the kitchen. He weighs in now at 260, and the family is afraid he may be addicted to mayonnaise on whole wheat with whatever's in the refrigerator.

Ever worry that you might be addicted to saliva? After all, if you don't swallow some every few minutes, your throat gets dry and scratchy.

Where does it end? That's the question, isn't it? Or more accurately, "Where does it begin?"

Anything that you come to *need* becomes an addiction. Some things hold a greater potential than others: caffeine, alcohol, cocaine, and sugar, for instance. Some substances are instantly addictive for some people. Crack cocaine is widely believed to be so lethal that users are hooked the very first time and spend the rest of their lives dying for the stuff. That would suggest that *any* use of such a substance is risky and constitutes abuse. Other substances may be enjoyed moderately. Sugar, for instance, can be safely consumed in small quantities and is a key ingredient in such delights as chocolate (which, as everyone knows, is the one addiction with which God is pleased).

Seriously: you can't abuse without being abused. Whatever the substance, it'll hound you until you're dog-tired, maybe dead.

We're left with a critical problem: where to play it safe and where to take a chance. The truest thing we can say right now is this: make your decisions about where to play it safe in the comfort of your own home. Don't wait till you're at a party or on a date.

See: Alcohol, Cocaine, Crystal, Saying No.

SUICIDE

A lot of people think suicide solves problems. It doesn't. All suicide does is kill you, and then you're dead. Suicide isn't romantic or heroic or easy. It is painful and final.

Some people are calling the current crop of high school students "a generation at risk." The image suggests the somber fear that if somebody doesn't do something, we could lose a lot of kids in the next few years. What are we supposed to do to stop that? How do we ease the pain—our own pain and the pain we see around us?

Tell the truth. A group of students responded to the question, "What would you say are the predominant emotions on your campus?" with a sobering list: loneliness, fear, pressure.

Most adults don't have a clue that anything like that might be true, so we've got to tell them. We've got to say without theatrics, "This is where it hurts." The adults we trust can't help it if they don't know.

Learn coping skills. Life doesn't have to be one crisis after another—but that's the way it is for a lot of people. Adolescence is a tough stretch no matter what. Physical, emotional, social, and intellectual changes gang up on us and sometimes make real mountains out of what should be molehills. You can learn to cut your mountains down to size by taking advantage of the resources within your reach.

Listen. "I know this is a permanent solution to a temporary problem," Frank said. He had lost his girlfriend and his dignity. "Nobody understands. People tell me I'll get over this—I'm young. I know that. But I need help *now*." Had it not been for the sensitivity of an assistant principal—had *she* not been listening to what he was getting at . . .

Act. Many airports now warn travelers that jokes about guns, bombs, or hijacking will be taken seriously. It's just as important to take seriously words and actions that suggest suicide, even if they seem like a joke. Most young suicides talk about it before they do it. If you hear or see something that makes you wonder, check it out and do something.

Pray. You're in the thick of this problem, but it's not *your* problem. Talking with God will give you the perspective you desperately need.

Offer Hope. Don't argue, don't deny anyone's feelings, but express hope with all the conviction you can muster. Any reason to hang in there may be reason enough. "You're gonna get through this and tomorrow we'll start putting things back together again. A *year* from now we'll look back on this and thank God we made it."

Stay put. If you think a friend is at risk, don't leave him alone.

Get help. A person contemplating suicide will most likely accept help right up to the last minute. If you think someone is at risk, take the initiative to get help. Don't let him talk you into keeping his intentions a secret. Be firm about this—it's hard but it's important. Take him to someone at school, to your youth worker, to a parent; get somebody involved who can understand the seriousness of the situation and take action. If you can't think of anything else, look in the front of the phone book for a crisis hot-line number.

Maintain confidentiality. If you can help someone through a crisis, that's wonderful! Once you've gotten help from a trusted adult, you've taken the story as far as it should go. Resist the temptation to spread the story, however innocently. Assuming your friend survives the crisis, he has to go on living. He doesn't need to hear his story told by someone who had nothing to do with it.

Follow through. Getting a person through the crisis is a beginning. What can you do to let them know that you're still there for them after the storm blows over?

More: Brent Q. Hafen and Kathryn J. Frandsen, *Youth Suicide: Depression and Loneliness* (Cordillera Press, 1986).

See: Depression, Friendship, Listening, Loneliness.

TECHNICAL VIRGINITY

Technical Virginity is a relatively new term floating around to describe people who are very experienced sexually, but who haven't "gone all the way" — and so consider themselves virgins. That may be technically true. A girl's hymen may be intact and a boy may never have inserted his penis into a vagina — but if a person has engaged in the kind of intimacy that produces an orgasm, then virginity is only a technicality.

So what's wrong with that?

First, it causes unsightly hair that grows along the spinal column so that wearing a bathing suit is out of the question. (Just kidding.) What it really causes is a kind of emotional and spiritual intimacy that normally accompanies giving yourself to another person as if you meant for it to be permanent. (See Serious.)

There are a lot of nice people who are creating sexual memories that'll be hard to forget later on, and nobody's bothered to tell them that it costs something to generate and then break intimacy of *any* kind.

147

Don't be talked into playing a game you'll lose on a technicality.

More: Romans 13:11-14.

See: Safe Sex, Sex.

TELEVISION

Maybe nobody ever told you TV can be bad for you. It can. On the other hand, maybe you've been

told that TV is *all* bad. It's not. Television may not be as bad as you think—or it may be worse. Some folks seem inclined to extremes way too much when it comes to watching TV. But it doesn't have to be so.

• Set high standards of quality for your TV viewing. If programming doesn't measure up, find something else to do.

• Don't turn it on just because it's there. Read a novel, write a novel, write a letter, bake a giant cookie.

• Don't watch TV for two weeks or a month just to see what you learn.

• Read the TV listings in advance and plan to watch *good* television.

• If you have a VCR, rent movies when there's nothing good on. Watch all the Academy Award Best-Picture winners in chronological order. (Use discretion—some winners are pretty rough.)

• Reruns are a waste of time, for the most part.

• If it sounded good in the listing but turns out to be a dog, turn it off. You don't have to watch to the bitter end.

• Don't let the people on TV keep you from paying attention to the people in your house.

• Don't believe everything you see. Especially don't buy the problem-solving models that dominate the tube.

• Use TV to relax, but not to escape.

• Be critical. Ask, "What do I like about this program? What's wrong with it? What would I do differently?"

More: Philippians 4:8.

VIOLENCE

Do you think you can watch fifty thousand violent acts on the screen and not be affected?
If you can, is that good news?
See: Rape.

WHEN YOU DON'T KNOW WHAT TO SAY

When you don't know what to say, don't say anything. Your friend's sister is killed in a car crash, your uncle has colon cancer, your favorite teacher loses her baby to crib death—and you don't know what to say. Maybe your attentive silence is better than talking at times like that. (See Listening.) You don't have to be—you can't be—an expert on everything, and that means there are times when all you can do is listen.

Writer and publisher Joe Bayly wrote about the loss of his child to leukemia and about the many nice folks who came to console him. Of all the people who expressed sympathy and understanding and "I know what you're going through," one stood out as a true comforter. That friend sat in a rocker across the room from Joe all night long, listening, quietly sharing Joe's tears, saying hardly a word. He had no advice, no stories, no encouragement. *He* was the friend who comforted Joe in his sorrow. Yet he said nothing.

See: Compassion, Listening.

WORK

See: Jobs.

WORSHIP

Worship isn't for you—it's for God. The plain, hard truth is that it doesn't matter if *you* get anything out of worship—though you always get more than you know. God gets something out of your worship even if it's grudging and sloppy and infantile. Like a patient father opening a badly wrapped gift—not a gift dad wanted, but some toy his child spotted at the mall and borrowed money from him to buy—like a patient, gracious, nurturing dad, God opens our worship. Worship is practice for the day when we see him as he is and it dawns on us what it means to be sons and daughters of the Almighty. If we make a little progress, catch a tiny glimpse of glory, offer one unselfish sacrifice of thanksgiving, perhaps we've moved a smidgen towards our humanity—for we were made to worship. Such little progress pries the word out of the noun form and into the active verb where it belongs.

For worship is a verb that comes from an ancient Greek word meaning *to kiss*. Worship is affection for the One we love. Following *worship* through its Latin roots, we track it to an Old English word, *worthship*. That's no lisp—worship is telling God how much he's worth according to your best estimate. What an extraordinary notion!

How much *is* God worth to you? How in the world are you going to express that to him?

More: Psalm 95; John 4:19-26.

See: Abba, Jesus, Yahweh.

YAHWEH

We began *Good Advice* with *Abba, Daddy*. You don't get much more intimate than *daddy*.

We end with *Yahweh* (YAW-way), *I am what I am*. You don't get much more remote than *I exist because I exist*.

Yahweh is the best guess at how the ancient Hebrews said the name of God.

If anything was clear to those ancient folks, it was that God was overwhelmingly other than human. The first five books of the Bible describe his power to create and save. The story of the Exodus was more than history—it was theology and hope in the God who reaches out with power to save his people. They were so awe-struck—maybe downright afraid—they determined that his name was too holy to speak, so they substituted the title *Lord* for his name. Some thought it too holy to even write, and eventually only the consonants were written and the vowels were literally lost (YHWH). If nothing else, they took God seriously.

From *Abba* to *Yahweh*. Anchoring the middle is Jesus, in whom God laid aside his otherness to become one of us.

What a wonder! *Abba* reminds us that God wants to be our daddy, to love and cherish us as sons and daughters. *Yahweh* reminds us that he has the power to do exactly that.